JWAIT

● Kuwait

IRAN

THE GULF

● Qatif

The Dahna

BAHRAIN

QATAR

● Hufuf

Ras Musandam

● Ras al-Khaimah

Sharjah ●

GULF OF OMAN

Riyadh

Abu Dhabi ●

● Bureimi

● Sib ● Muscat

TRUCIAL
STATES

● Ibri

Jabal Akhdar

● Bani bu Ali

Ramlah al Ghafa

MUSCAT
&
OMAN

Rub al-Khali (The Empty Quarter)

Dhofar

● Dhofar

ARABIAN SEA

SOUTHERN YEMEN

Wadi Hadhramaut

Shibam ● ● Tarim

dhramaut ● Saiyun

● Sayhut

● As Shihr
Mukalla

GULF OF ADEN

SOCOTRA

Travellers in Arabia

Hamlyn
London New York Sydney Toronto

Travellers in
Arabia
Robin Bidwell

Dedication

To my Arab friends who have
made my days in their land among
the most enjoyable of my life.

Title page illustration:
The hillside town of Kohlan in the
Yemen.

Published by
The Hamlyn Publishing Group Limited
London New York Sydney Toronto
Astronaut House
Hounslow Road
Feltham, Middlesex

© Copyright
The Hamlyn Publishing Group Limited 1976

ISBN 0 600 32900 3

Filmset by Keyspools Limited, Golborne,
Lancs.

Printed by Leefung-Asco Printers Ltd,
Hong Kong

Contents

Introduction

PROBABLY THERE is more written about Arabia than on any other part of the world and the literature varies from the 600,000 words of Doughty to brief articles in learned journals. My selection for this book was therefore bound to be subjective: I could only put in what seemed to me interesting, amusing or important and hope that the reader will agree with my choice. It has been necessary to omit many who have made great contributions to knowledge of Arabia: solid works on botany or geology do not make easy reading. I have written this mainly to please myself and can only hope that my enjoyment will be communicated to others.

There are things in this book which may not please my Arab friends, but I must point out to them that in a work such as this I am not entirely my own master. If a traveller disapproved of the rites of the Pilgrimage or was maltreated by unpleasant Beduins, I can only record the fact while saying that my own experiences have been very different. I have enormous respect for the integrity of the genuine Muslim and have had great enjoyment from the companionship of Arabs of all classes. I am sure that the Arabs have sufficient maturity and self-confidence not to take offence where none is intended.

I am very fond of sixteenth or seventeenth-century English spelling and have retained it wherever I could. The question of the transliteration of Arabic is the pet province of the pompous pedant. I know that in academic circles one should write 'Abd al-'Azīz ibn 'Abd al-Raḥmān ibn Sa'ūd but I am convinced that the ordinary reader does not want to be bothered with 'these damned dots and dashes': I have therefore written personal names as simply as possible. For place names, where there is a version familiar to English people – for example Jedda – I have used that, otherwise I have used *The Times Atlas*, omitting dots and dashes.

Robin Bidwell
Middle East Centre
Cambridge

A map of Arabia printed in Paris in 1683. Many of the names – and all the rivers – are imaginary.

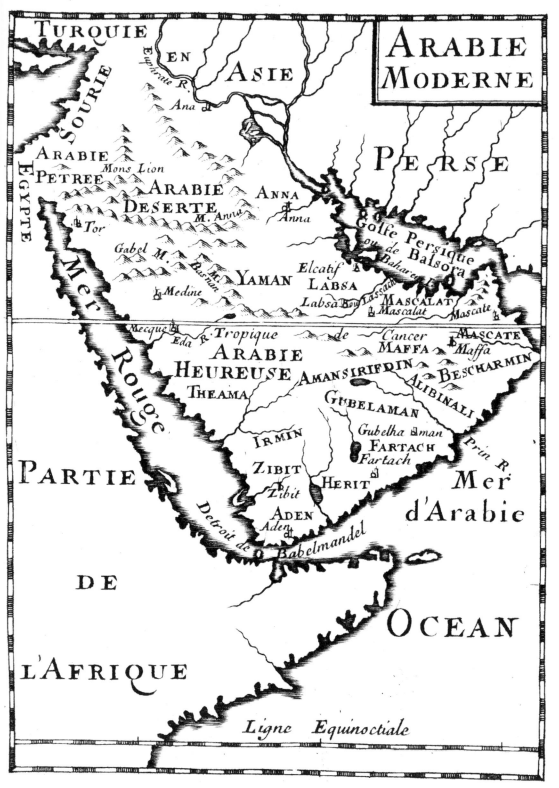

ARABIE MODERNE

TURQUIE EN ASIE

SOURIE

ASSOURIE

EGYPTE

Euphrate R.

Ana

PERSE

ARABIE PETREE

Mons Lion

ARABIE DESERTE

M. Anna

ANNA

Anna

Anna

Tor

Gabel M.

Basman

YAMAN

Elcatif

LABSA

Golfe Persique ou de Balsora

Bahareu

Medine

Labsa Bou Lassach

MASCALAT

Mascalat

Mascate

Mecque

Eda

R. Tropique de Cancer

MASCATE

Mer Rouge

ARABIE HEUREUSE

MAFFA

Maffa

BESCHARMIN

THEAMA

AMANSIRIFDIN

ALIBINALI

GUBELAMAN

IRMIN

Gubelha Aman

FARTACH

Prin R.

ZIBIT

Fartach

Zibit

HERIT

Mer d'Arabie

ADEN

Aden

PARTIE

Detroit de Babelmandel

DE

OCEAN

L'AFRIQUE

Ligne Equinoctiale

7

Arabia

To SET the stage upon which our travellers moved, it is necessary to say a few words about the geography and history of Arabia. This short survey will deal mainly with the area that is now the Kingdom of Saudi Arabia – particulars about the south-east and the south-west of the peninsula will emerge in the appropriate chapters.

The Arabian peninsula covers about a million square miles with a maximum length of 1400 miles and a maximum width of 1200. Along the western coast there is a fairly narrow plain rising steeply to mountains, some of which are nearly 10,000 feet in height. This area is the Hejaz. Beyond the ranges is Nejd, which is basically a plateau sloping gradually eastwards until it reaches the Persian Gulf, where it vanishes into a series of salty marshes often indistinguishable from the sea.

The core of the country is the crescent-shaped escarpment of Jabal Tuwayq on which is to be found much of the 1 per cent of the land which is cultivable and a series of towns including Riyadh, Unayzah and Buraydah. West of this crescent lies the area of Harras – a huge extent of black lava, often standing ten feet straight out of the sandy waste. Girdling the crescent on the northern, eastern and southern sides is sheer sandy desert. To the north is the Nafud, covering perhaps 26,000 square miles; then comes the Dahna about 400 miles long and about 30 wide and this merges into the Empty Quarter, the Rub al-Khali, the greatest desert of all. This covers about 200,000 square miles, a surface greater than that of France, and is a mass of dunes rising often to 500 feet. Much of the Peninsula that is neither sand nor mountain is hard gravel and flinty soil which could be cultivated if only there were enough water.

Most of Arabia gets some rainfall every year, but only in the coastal strips of the west, south and south-east is it heavy and regular. Any part may, however, suffer a sudden flood which comes roaring down the normally dry wadis as a wall of water perhaps six feet high, travelling faster than a man may run and bearing with it trees, animals and even an occasional vehicle if anyone has been foolhardy enough to leave one unattended. The floods can be extensive: once the courtyard of the Great Mosque at Mecca was under ten feet of water, and a famous tale recounts how a conqueror took advantage of heavy rain to turn the Mosque at Sanaa in the Yemen into an open-air swimming pool in which the local damsels were obliged to bathe naked. There is, however, nothing that a European would call either a river or a lake.

It is unnecessary to stress the heat of Arabia but it is important to realise that at night it can be terribly cold. Philby found places where the variation between day and night temperature was 40 degrees. A personal experience may illustrate the contrasts of the country. In the heat and humidity of an Aden morning, this writer could wear a shirt only for a quarter of an hour before it became too wet and sticky to endure: he spent the night a hundred miles away 8000 feet in the mountains and shivered under fourteen blankets.

History

Within a century of the death of the Prophet Muhammad in AD 632 and the unique outburst of energy when Arab arms carried their new faith to the Atlantic and to the boundaries of China, the peninsula had become a backwater. Almost its only source of wealth was the *Haj* – the pilgrimage to Mecca that the Prophet had enjoined upon all those of his followers who were able to make it. The Hejaz has never been able to feed itself and has depended heavily upon grain from Egypt – to which it was frequently a political appendage. This was the case throughout the Middle Ages when the Meccans acknowledged the overlordship of the Sultans of Egypt, whose position was further enhanced by their giving refuge to

the Khalifs who had fled from Baghdad at the Mongol invasion.

The Khalif, the 'Successor' of the Prophet, was not the only great religious figure in the Islamic world; in Mecca resided the Grand Sharif, the head of all the direct descendants of Muhammad. Naturally he enjoyed enormous prestige and was greatly venerated by the Arab tribes of the Hejaz.

In 1517 the Ottomans conquered Egypt and proclaimed the Hejaz part of their dominions. The Grand Sharif sent his son to do homage to the victor, Selim the Grim, and to present him with a Quran supposedly written by the second Khalif and a silver key to the Kaabah. At the same time the Turk carried off to Constantinople the mantle and banner of the Prophet which the Khalifs had taken to Cairo. The Sultan in Constantinople assumed the title of Protector of the Holy Places: his successors later claimed the Khalifate.

The Turkish Sultan thus gained the religious leadership of Islam and accepted the responsibility of ensuring the

Arabian contrasts. The dunes at the edges of the Empty Quarter, and the majestic mountains on the frontier between Saudi Arabia and the Yemen. It was in these mountains that the Imam of Badr established his headquarters in the war which lasted from 1962 to 1967.

10

safety of the pilgrimage, with garrisons installed at strategic points along the route under the control of Pashas in Mecca and Medina. Apart from this they made no real attempt to rule Arabia and indeed much nearer home their control was practically non-existent. Within a century of the conquest effective power in Cairo and Baghdad was in the hands of local officers who paid formal tribute to the Sultan but tolerated no interference from him. By the end of the eighteenth century a Governor of Aleppo was regarded as an exceptionally strong man because he could keep order up to an hour's ride from the city gates, while the lunatic Jazzar Pasha in Acre could gouge out eyes and nail the tongues of lying shopkeepers to their counters without any comment from his sovereign. The Ottoman Government stood by while its Governors in Syrian provinces made war upon one another, not always displeased that they should thus dissipate their energies. It was when one nominally Turkish vassal, Muhammad Ali, whose seizure of power as Pasha of Egypt the Sultan had ratified willy-nilly, became really strong that Constantinople suffered its greatest humiliation. In 1831 Muhammad Ali sent his son Ibrahim to invade Syria, and his advance took him almost to the shores of the Bosphorus before the great powers of Europe intervened to secure his withdrawal. It was those same great powers that were inexorably lopping off province after province from a European empire which had once extended almost to the walls of Vienna, included parts of Poland and the Ukraine, and could claim the Black Sea as an entirely Turkish lake.

Internally, there was a rigid conservatism and an arrogant conviction that Turkish Muslims had nothing to learn from barbarian unbelievers; they allowed the technological progress that had started to sweep through western Europe to pass them by. Not a single book had ever been translated into Turkish, and at the end of the eighteenth century it was said that there was not a single person within the ruling establishment who had heard of Galileo. The suggestion of the formation of a fire-brigade was denounced as an impious attempt to interfere with the will of God, and the highest religious authorities declared that Allah would never bless an army which appeared in trousers. Strongest of all forces against change were the Janissaries, once the crack troops who had been the first into every battle but now a hereditary mob of gangsters who could only be stirred into action by the fear of losing their privileges.

In such circumstances, the Ottoman Government had little time to spare for events in Arabia. As far as it had any objective beyond the mere continuation of its own existence, it was dedicated to ensuring the practice of Islam and it took a major attack by Beduin robbers on the pilgrimage of 1757, when 20,000 *hajjis* were said to have died of thirst in the desert after their transport had been stolen, to make the Turks bestir themselves a little in the Hejaz. They had not the slightest interest in Nejd where there was no authority of any sort – a confusion of Beduin tribes and tiny villages all of which were independent and usually at war with one another.

One of these hamlets, situated some seven miles from the present city of Riyadh, was called Diriyyah and had been ruled since the sixteenth century by the family of Ibn Saud.

In 1745 Muhammad ibn Saud gave refuge to a religious judge whose zeal in applying the law in its totality had led to threats to his life. Muhammad ibn Abd al-Wahhab was a passionate enthusiast who believed that all the faults of the time had arisen from the abandoning of the pure practices of their ancestors. Every innovation since the days of the Prophet, even smoking or drinking coffee, was sinful and wrong: worst of all innovations was the popular belief that saints, and even Muhammad, could serve as mediators between God and Man. There were still numerous traces of pre-Islamic paganism in Nejd, the worship of stones and trees – even more damnable.

Muhammad ibn Abd al-Wahhab persuaded the whole population of Diriyyah from Ibn Saud downwards that all who differed from him were infidels, non-Muslims indeed, against whom it was a duty to conduct the holy war (*jihad*) and whose property ought to be seized for the benefit of the faithful. Few things are more welcome than a licence to loot in the name of religion, and his followers, called by themselves Unitarians and by their opponents Wahhabis, took full advantage of it with twenty-five campaigns in five years. Soon after 1800 they had smashed up the most sacred tombs in Iraq, carrying off enormous booty, and their raiding parties had reached as far north as Aleppo. Both these areas were of course still nominally part of the Ottoman Empire. In the meantime their influence reached the Gulf and the joyous duty of despoiling the infidel by sea was undertaken by the tribes of what soon became known as the Pirate Coast.

The head of the house of Ibn Saud, Abd al-Aziz, assumed the title of Imam, Leader of the Faithful, and it was inevitable that he should clash with the Grand Sharif of Mecca for each regarded the other as a dangerous heretic. There were several skirmishes before, in the summer of 1802, Abd al-Aziz ibn Saud captured the Holy City where he executed a few of the more obnoxious religious doctors before withdrawing. In 1806 his son Saud reoccupied Mecca and captured Medina, allowing both cities to be looted. He prevented pilgrims from coming from the north, alleging that they were not authentic Muslims. This at last stung the Ottoman Empire into action and the Sultan Mahmud II, asked his vassal, Muhammad Ali Pasha of Egypt, to intervene. In 1811 a Turco-Egyptian force drove the Nejdis out of Mecca and Medina. The campaign proved long and difficult and it was not until seven years later that the Pasha's son Ibrahim succeeded in capturing the Saudi capital of Diriyyah, which he reduced to the ruin that it is today. Abdallah ibn Saud, who succeeded his father in 1814, was put to death in Constantinople.

Selim the Grim, the ninth Ottoman Sultan, deposed his father in 1512, and his first action was to exterminate his relatives. He was a distinguished poet and his letters to the Shah of Persia are masterpieces of elegance: they were, however, so insulting that his messengers were executed. In 1517 he conquered Egypt. His reign and that of his son Suleiman the Magnificent (succeeded 1520) represent the greatest period of the Ottoman Empire.

The Egyptians decided to concentrate their forces in the Hejaz and to leave a puppet ruler in Nejd, which they had so devastated that they thought that there was little chance of its ever troubling them again. Although most of the princes of the House of Saud had been taken into exile, one of them, Turki ibn Abdallah escaped and raised the standard of revolt. He recaptured Riyadh and managed to bring much of Nejd back under the control of his family. In May 1834 Turki was murdered by a kinsman who ruled for forty days until Turki's son Faysal climbed into the palace and cut the usurper's throat.

Faysal's companion in this enterprise was a chief from Hail in Jabal Shammar, Abdallah ibn Rashid, who was already a figure of legend. After a battle he had been left for dead with a huge gash in his neck but locusts had appeared and with their wings scuffed sand into the wound while a disciplined flock of birds hovered above to keep off the sun. Faysal appointed Abdallah as Emir of his native province as a reward for his help.

In 1838 the Egyptians advanced again, captured Faysal and took him into exile in Cairo. In 1840, however, all their expansionist policies collapsed as a result of the implacable hostility of Lord Palmerston and they withdrew from Arabia, installing a renegade Saudi prince as ruler of Nejd. Early in 1843 Faysal, who had escaped from his prison, reappeared and with the help of Abdallah ibn Rashid had little difficulty in regaining his throne.

Abdallah ibn Rashid was succeeded by his son Talal as Emir of Jabal Shammar. Talal continued to present himself as a respectful vassal of the Imam Faysal but in

Abdallah ibn Saud succeeded his father in 1814, three years after the Egyptian invasion of Arabia had started. In 1818 his capital was destroyed and he himself taken a captive to Constantinople where he was executed and his head crushed in a mortar.

practice became more and more independent. He extended his influence throughout northern Arabia by showing the virtues that the Arabs most admire, generosity, courage and justice. He continued to profess his loyalty to Faysal's successor Abdallah but in 1867, fearing that he was going mad, he shot himself.

Talal was followed by his brother Mtab who, after a reign of four years, was murdered by his nephews with, so legend says, a specially forged silver bullet. The elder, Bandar, assumed power but lasted only a few months before he, too, was cut down by another of Talal's brothers. This was Muhammad ibn Rashid who was to dominate northern and eastern Arabia for more than a quarter of a century.

In the meantime Saud, the younger son of Faysal, had revolted against his brother Abdallah and installed himself in Riyadh. The Turks from Iraq took advantage of the fratricidal strife to occupy the easternmost province of Nejd – the Hasa. Saud died of smallpox in 1875 and Abdallah returned to power – but soon found that he could maintain himself only with the help of Muhammad ibn Rashid who came to dominate him completely. When in 1887 Abdallah was unable to cope with a revolt of his nephews, Ibn Rashid occupied Riyadh and drove the family into exile.

Muhammad ibn Rashid was one of the rare members of his dynasty to die in his bed and he was succeeded by his nephew Abd al-Aziz. The latter soon found himself confronted by the greatest warrior that Arabia had produced for a thousand years. This was another Abd al-Aziz, better known as the great Ibn Saud who, in January 1902 at the age of eighteen, recaptured Riyadh with seven companions. In April 1906, after several battles, Ibn Saud defeated and killed Abd al-Aziz ibn Rashid who was succeeded by his eighteen-year-old son. This lad lasted until January 1907 when he was treacherously murdered by two of his cousins. The elder ruled for a year before the younger one killed him, to survive for almost a year before he was himself assassinated. One of the few survivors of the family, a boy of ten, was proclaimed Emir, with a Regent who was poisoned shortly afterwards.

15

The great Ibn Saud in 1917, when he was in his late thirties. With him are two people who made their mark as Arabian travellers—Sir Percy Cox and Gertrude Bell.

This Emir managed to survive for a decade before he was shot by a cousin whom he had injudiciously challenged to target practice. The murderer was instantly slaughtered by a slave and another cousin mounted the throne so unwillingly that at the first opportunity he bolted to safety with Ibn Saud. His successor proved the last of the thirteen Emirs who had ruled during the ninety very troubled years of Jabal Shammar's independence; in November 1921 Ibn Saud captured Hail and took the remnants of the family to Riyadh as honoured guests in palaces that they were not permitted to leave.

While his rivals were thus tearing themselves apart, Ibn Saud was consolidating his position. After 1912 he had an extraordinary weapon – the dreaded Ikhwan. The Ikhwan were communities of Beduins that he settled and then deliberately fanaticised by sending among them preachers to drive home the message that all outside their ranks were heretics beyond the law whom it was their duty to attack. They lived in the most puritan austerity and their main hope was to achieve Paradise by dying in a holy war. Their practice was to fire their rifles once and then to charge with the sword and few could resist them. Early in 1914 they bundled the Turks out of the Hasa in a matter of days.

In November 1914 Britain and Turkey went to war and

This fifteenth-century picture shows how little was known about Arabia in Europe. It does seem improbable, however, that people should have thought camel-drivers were naked simians with tails!

the English aimed to use discontented Arabs against their Ottoman masters. There was a debate in Whitehall as to whether Ibn Saud or Sharif Hussain of Mecca would prove the better ally but contact was lost with the former. The Foreign Office preferred anyway to deal with the more sophisticated Meccans whose leaders, unlike Ibn Saud, knew something of the world outside Arabia. In addition it felt that only the prestige of the Sharif could nullify the call of the Sultan for a Holy War which might set the Muslims of India alight. The Arab Revolt broke out in June 1916 and in November 1918 the Sharifian army just outpaced the British into Damascus.

Even before and during the war there had been clashes between the Ikhwan and the Sharifians, and these continued. For some time there was the macabre situation in which Ibn Saud's men fired rifles, obtained through the India Office, at Hussain's troops who replied with weapons provided by the Foreign Office. In intervals between these skirmishes, Ibn Saud added Jabal Shammar, the northern oases of Jawf and the great Wadi Sirhan to his dominions, bringing his frontiers up to the new British Mandates of Iraq and Transjordan.

In the summer of 1924 there was a final quarrel between the rulers of Hejaz and Nejd. Ibn Saud let loose the Ikhwan who soon captured Taif where they perpetrated an appalling massacre, adding still more to the terror of their name. In October they took Mecca but Ibn Saud was on hand to prevent any more atrocities. Hussain, who had proclaimed himself Khalif and King of the Arabs, abdicated and fled. His successor, his son Ali, ruled little more than the city of Jedda and that too fell before the end of 1925. The state was to reach its present limits with the absorption of the province of Asir in the south-west and finally, after a war with the Yemen, with the annexation of Najran in 1934.

In January 1926 Ibn Saud was proclaimed King of the Hejaz and Nejd, a title which he changed in 1932 to that of King of Saudi Arabia. The details of his reign are beyond the scope of this book, but some will emerge in the accounts of contemporary travellers which make up the later chapters.

Europe discovers the Middle East

DURING THE early Middle Ages relations between Christian and Muslim were not unfriendly: Harun al-Rashid presented Charlemagne with an elephant and a future Pope realised that the best education in the world was to be found in Fez. An English saint, Willibald, visited Jerusalem and was only mildly rebuked when he was caught smuggling. This peaceful co-existence ended towards the end of the eleventh century when for a variety of reasons, political, economic and possibly even religious, the leaders of Christendom embarked upon the Crusades. After these wars there was such hostility that Dante was prepared to put Muhammad in the lowest reaches of Hell. A few points of friendly contact remained but even these vanished as the brutish Turks established their domination over the Middle East.

Lady Mary Wortley Montagu (1689–1762) was a famous letter writer whose accounts of the East convey its atmosphere and show unusual sympathy for Islam. She introduced vaccination against small-pox into England. A tempestuous character, she traded insults with Swift and Pope and conducted a series of dramatic love affairs.

The first part of the sixteenth century was a time of particularly bitter conflict as the Portuguese thrust their way into seas of which the Muslims had held the monopoly but this period did not last for long. Before 1600 there were English and French Ambassadors in Constantinople and Merchant Companies trading with Egypt and the Levant. There was a large British community at Aleppo, some of whose members took an intellectual interest in the world around them. Scholars like George Sandys wrote about Beduins and camels for the educated man at home. In the hope that Muslims might be saved, a Professorship of Arabic was created at Cambridge in 1632.

Other universities followed and the first Professor at Oxford started a collection of oriental manuscripts, arranging them to be printed 200 years before there was a press in Egypt. In 1652 a Polyglot Bible which included Arabic was presented to Cromwell. Early in the next century what is still probably the best translation of the Quran into English appeared and so did a French version of the *Arabian Nights*.

Then travel became easier, and young nobles on the Grand Tour started to go on from Italy to Egypt and Turkey, where from 1717 the sparkling Lady Mary Wortley Montagu was Ambassadress. In 1721 there was what was probably the first exhibition of a Pharaonic figure at the Society of Antiquaries and about 1740 an Egyptian Society met regularly at a tavern in Chandos Street with Lord Sandwich as its 'Sheich'.

Writers such as Samuel Johnson and Voltaire began to set their tales in an imaginary Orient while Montesquieu used the device of a visiting Persian to satirize his own country. Then philosophers such as Rousseau and Swedenborg started to find merits in the Quran.

By the end of the eighteenth century it was not uncommon to go to India overland through Egypt or Syria, and, naturally, men's imaginations were interested in the lands which bordered this no longer adventurous route. Byron and Moore enchanted the young with romantic pictures of an idealised Orient. Men became more interested in themselves and their own reactions and travellers' tales start to change from the severely factual to blendings with impressions and imagination.

As the nineteenth century progressed, life became so ordered and secure that certain temperaments began to yearn for the open desert horizons and the free wandering life of the Beduin. Their picture was Utopian but as Europe became ever more bourgeois and materialist, so the Middle East seemed to stand out in starker contrast. For some, unsure of their place in society, to travel became a spiritual quest for different and better values. Arabia was a place where some went to discover themselves: many returned transformed.

Three Travellers to Mecca

... IF ANY man shall demaunde of me the cause of this my vyage, certeynely I can shewe no better reason then is the ardent desire of Knowledge, which hath moved many other to see the worlde and the miracles of God therin. And forasmuch as other knowen partes of the world, have heretofore ben sufficiently traveyled of other, I was determyned to visite and describe suche partes as here before have not been sufficiently knowen' – so starts the English translation of the Navigations of Lewes Vertomannus or Ludovico de Varthema, 'Gentleman of the citie of Rome'. He certainly succeeded in his ambition for he has left us the earliest European account of the pilgrimage to Mecca, the first description of the Spice Islands, east of Java, and was probably also the first to give even a hearsay mention of Australia.

It was in December 1502 that he left Venice and after a short visit to Egypt, arrived the following spring in Damascus. There he met a Christian renegade, now an officer in the Ottoman forces who agreed to take him to Mecca as one of the troops escorting the pilgrimage. There were some sixty soldiers to guard 35,000 camels and 40,000 men. Varthema had obviously the fine swashbuckling spirit of a true Renaissance Italian for he describes a battle against marauding Beduins in which his side lost a man and a woman killed but 'we slue of the Arabians a thousande and fyve hundred, whereof you neede not marveyle, if you consider that they are unarmed, and wear only a thynne loose vesture, and are besydes almost naked'. Varthema was always less interested in places than in oddities and spends little time in describing the holy cities of Mecca and Medina before

Ludovico de Varthema is the only traveller to have claimed to have seen unicorns in the Great Mosque at Mecca. His description roughly resembles this sixteenth-century drawing.

hurrying on to look at something else.

An example of this may be found in his chapter entitled 'the unicorns of the temple of Mecca, not very common in other places'. He recounts that the beast 'is of the coloure of a horse of weesell coloure, and hath the head like an hart, but no long necke, a thynne mane, hangyng only on the one syde: theyr legges are thyn and slender, lyke a fawne or hynde: the hoofes of the fore feete are divided in two, much like the feet of a Goat, the outwarde part of the hynder feete is very full of heare. This beast doubtlesse seemeth wylde and fierce, yet tempereth that fiercenesse with a certain comelinesse'. He was told that they were a gift from the King of Ethiopia.

Varthema determined to continue his travels and not to return to Damascus with the caravan. His Captain, in return for help with a smuggling venture, connived at his desertion and he lay hidden until his companions had departed. From Jedda he embarked for Aden, the crew tarrying only to land and plunder the village of Jizan when they found that their supplies were running low.

Varthema had escaped from the forbidden Hejaz but his troubles were only about to begin. 'The day after our arryvyng [at Aden], the Mahumetans tooke mee, and put shackles on my legges, which came by occasion of a certain Idolatour who cryed after mee, saying O Christian Dogge, borne of Dogges. When the Mahumetans hearde the name of a Christian, incontinent they layde handes on mee' and demanded that he should be put to death as a spy. The Governor of Aden lacked the power to do this so, loading him with heavy chains, despatched him to the Sultan of Yemen.

Varthema decided to escape by feigning madness but this 'weryed me so muche that I was never so tyred with laboure or greeved with payne', for 'the boyes and rascall people sometyme to the number of 40 or 50 hurled stones at me almost without ceassing'. In the character of religious zeal he converted a 'great fatt sheepe' to Islam and put to death a donkey which had neglected to praise the Prophet. Finally two learned men were brought to investigate whether Varthema was 'a holy man or a madde man. They were also of divers opinions, some affyrming one thyng, and some another. While they were yet debatying this matter for the space of an houre, I pyssed in my hands, hurlde it in theyr faces; whereby they agreed that I was no Sainct, but a mad man'.

Relief, however, was at hand, for to demonstrate his madness, Varthema, according to his tale, which may well be untrue, was in the habit of standing nearly naked by the window. He caught the eye of the 'Queen' (Sultana) herself and learned that 'the women of Arabia are greatly in love with whyte men'. She laughed at his pranks, sent him food and came frequently to visit him, lamenting that

Medina, from Mallet's *Description de l'Univers* of 1683. De Varthema and the guards of the pilgrimage may well have resembled the soldiers shown here entering Medina.

22

she and all her family were black while he was as white as the sun. Varthema was starting to wonder how to extricate himself from so embarrassing a situation but eventually he managed to persuade her to let him go for a cure to a reputed miracle-worker in Aden. There he wasted no time in boarding a ship. The date was March 1504 and he had been in Arabia for about ten months.

At this point, regretfully, we must take leave of Varthema. It would have been fun to have gone on with him to the Indies which he reached a mere six years after Vasco da Gama, to have met with him the King who tied his moustaches in a bow over his head, and the tribe who had 'cruell maners in selling their parents to the Anthropophagi to be eaten'. It would have been agreeable to have dwelt on 'The Chapter showing how elephants generate' – he found them 'of all foure footed beastes, and nexte unto man, the most wittie and docible, not farre from human sence'. However these matters are beyond the scope of this book, and we can only say that after adventures in Persia, the East Indies, Ethiopia and Mozambique, he returned to Rome in the winter of 1508–9. His book appeared with a dedication to an Italian Duchess and nothing more is known about him. Perhaps he was murdered for raising his eyes above his station.

Varthema's account is the brisk narrative of a man of action – little interested in details of topography or of the practices of worship at Mecca, which anyway he lacked the background to put in perspective. It was, however, to remain the only account readily available in a European language for nearly 200 years until Joseph Pitts published in 1704 'A Faithful Account of the Religion and Manners of the Mahometans . . . with an account of the Author's being taken captive, the Turks' cruelty to him and his escape.' This book gave the first drawing of the Mosque at Mecca (it reminded the author of the Royal Exchange) and the first detailed account of the ceremonies of the pilgrimage.

Joseph Pitts was born in Exeter about 1663, the son of a pious Dissenter. He went to sea and on almost his first voyage was captured by Algerian corsairs. Writing forty years later he still recalled the horror of that moment – 'I being but Young, the Enemy seem'd to me as monstrous ravenous Creatures, which made me cry out, O, Master, I am afraid they will kill us and eat us. No, no Child, said my Master, they will carry us to Algier and sell us.' This proved true and Pitts' first owner or Patroon used regularly to beat the soles of his feet, pausing from time to time to restore his strength by enjoying a peaceful hubble-bubble.

After some time he was sold to a second Patroon who determined to convert him to Islam – if necessary by thrashing. 'I roar'd out,' wrote Pitts, 'to feel the pain of his cruel strokes, but the more I cry'd the more furiously he laid on and to stop the Noise of my crying would stamp with his feet on my mouth.' Despite the fact that at long intervals letters arrived from his father telling him, from the safety of Devon, never to renounce the true faith, one can hardly blame Pitts for making a formal profession of Islam. He secretly hated his new religion and 'ate heartily in private of hog'. There was one difficult test of his

The 'standing' on Mount Arafat which Joseph Pitts found so emotionally moving. The pilgrims, numbering many thousands, are all clad in the *ihram,* the simple, obligatory garment which makes it impossible to distinguish rich from poor – for all men are equal in the sight of God.

conversion for at Alexandria he was confronted with 'a pillar of stone, unpolish'd which looked not much unlike the stump of a dead tree, with knots on it'. This was reputed to be the very fig tree that Christ had cursed and rendered barren and if anyone could walk blind-fold straight towards it from ten yards, it was clear that he was a genuine Muslim. Fortunately Pitts passed the test.

After his second Patroon lost his head plotting against the Dey of Algiers, Pitts was sold to an old bachelor who treated him more like a Jeeves than a slave. Probably in 1685 they went on the pilgrimage together and it was on this journey that the incident just described took place. He gives an interesting, if not highly original account of Cairo – he noted that 'Egyptians scold like whores, but seldom care to fight', and that they enjoyed cheating people who were uncertain of the coinage. The pair went on to Suez, boarded a ship and about a month later arrived at Jedda.

After assuming the garb of the pilgrim – the *ihram* – 'many times enduring the scorching heat of the sun until their very skin is burnt off their backs and arms and their heads swoll'n to a very great degree', they reached Mecca. He was determined, like many another Englishman abroad, not to be impressed and thought Mecca 'a little ragged town' and though he twice entered the Kaabah 'I found nothing worth seeing in it'. The locals were unworthy of regard being 'a poor sort of people, very thin, lean and swarthy'. He went through the rites of the *haj* but despite himself 'I profess I could not chuse but admire to see those poor creatures so extraordinarily devout and affectionate when they were about these superstitions, and with what awe and trembling they were possess'd: insomuch that I could scarce forbear shedding of tears to see their zeal, tho' blind and idolatrous.' He was also greatly moved by the ceremonies on Mount Arafat (not in itself, of course, a mountain of the slightest interest): 'It was a sight, indeed, able to pierce one's heart to behold so many thousands, in their garments of humility and mortification, with their naked heads and cheeks watered with tears, and to hear their grievous sighs and sobs, begging earnestly for the

One of the last pictures of Mecca contrived from hearsay before it was accurately described by Ali Bey and Burckhardt. Engraved in 1790, it shows a great improvement over earlier efforts.

remission of their sins.'

Pitts and his Patroon returned to Cairo by land by way of Medina which, hardly surprisingly, he thought 'a little town and poor'. His worst expectations were probably realised when his Patroon was robbed of a silk handkerchief while actually praying at the tomb of the Prophet ('the dead jugler' as Pitts would have it). After another thirty days' journey, seeing no green thing nor beast nor fowl they reached Egypt to find that the plague had the country in its grip. At Alexandria Pitts caught the disease but managed, he says, to cure it by roasting an onion and applying it dipped in oil to his sores. In the city he met an old school friend and sent home by him presents to his parents.

Pitts and his Patroon returned to Algiers. Pitts was no longer a slave, having been formally liberated at Mecca, but he was supposed to be a Muslim and any attempt to renounce the faith was punishable by death. It was some seven years before he had an opportunity to escape, enlisting in the Turkish navy and deserting in Smyrna. He made his way back to England and on his first night he was seized by a Press Gang for service in the Royal Navy. He managed to get himself released and reached home in 1693 and with his father knelt to give thanks for his return. He then seems to have lived quietly in Exeter for another forty years.

Pitts spent about fifteen years in the Arab world and, as a nominal Muslim, had obviously considerable knowledge of that faith. His tale is that of an honest Englishman, full of prejudices and distrust of foreigners but is accurate and truthful. It seems to have remained almost entirely unread.

Varthema, the first traveller in this chapter, went to Mecca as the escort of a caravan and the second, Pitts, as a slave: the third, Ali Bey el-Abbassi went as a prince, a descendant of the great family of Khalifs which had included Harun al-Rashid. Rarely can an account of a journey started with the author giving less information about himself – there is a short prayer in Arabic and the statement, 'After having passed many years in the Christian states, studying there the sciences of nature, and the arts most useful to man in society . . . I determined at last to visit the Mahometan countries; and while engaged in performing a pilgrimage to Mecca, to observe the manners, customs, and nature of the countries through which I should pass, in order that I might make the laborious journey of some utility to the country which I might at last select for my abode.'

Ali Bey's tale, then, starts abruptly with his disembarkation at Tangier in June 1803. The picture that he gives of Morocco is beyond the scope of this work, but it is important to establish the impression that he gives of his own grandeur. He became a personal friend of the Sultan to whom, amongst other things, he presented twenty muskets with bayonets, a barrel of gunpowder and a handsome umbrella. In return he received two black loaves from the Sultan's own oven – a sign of brotherhood. More practically, 'the Sultan made me a present of some considerable estates, which, independently of my own funds, enabled me to maintain the expenses which my rank required', and sent him also two second-hand ladies from his own harem.

After two years, Ali Bey set out on his pilgrimage, calling at Tripoli where the Pasha implored him to stay, and at Cyprus where all the Bishops hastened to wait upon him to pay their respects. Pausing a while at Cairo, where, of course, he was received by Muhammad Ali himself, he set out with the caravan for Suez on 15 December 1806. 'My part of the cavalcade was composed of 14 camels and 3 horses only; for I had left almost all my effects, and a number of my servants in Egypt.' Two of his staff used to ride ahead and prepare picnics for him.

Ali Bey as he represented himself. From an engraving published in 1814.

He embarked on a dhow which reminded him of ancient Trojan galleys and which a fortnight later ran aground during the night: 'we all thought that we were lost, and uttered cries of desolation and despair. In the midst of these clamours I distinguished the shrill voice of a man, who sobbed and cried like a child. I asked who it was, and found it to be the captain'. Ali Bey commandeered a small boat and organised the rowing by singing to the oarsmen. After three hours they reached the coast of Arabia, where some hours later they were rescued by their own ship. They all embraced and wept in each others' arms.

On 23 January 1807 Ali Bey entered Mecca and was accommodated in a house adjoining that of the Grand Sharif which had been prepared for him in advance. Soon he was received by the Sharif, whom he told that he was from Aleppo, and who sought his advice on world affairs. As a special mark of distinction, the Sharif appointed a high official to accompany him in his wanderings around the city: this was the Keeper of the Holy Well of Zemzem who bore the subsidiary title of The Poisoner. They became great friends but Ali Bey always carried a powerful emetic in his pocket.

Ali Bey was the first to give the West a systematic account of Mecca, the first to describe its trade, fauna and flora and even the first to fix its exact position. He found that large parts of the city were ruined and that the population had shrunk from at least 100,000 to a mere 16,000. He thought that there was no city with less craftsmanship: there was no gunsmith, lockmaker or cobbler and it was impossible to buy a well-written or even a correct Quran. It is little wonder that he regarded the inhabitants as 'the most ignorant of mortals'. On the other hand, he never saw such bold mice, who danced and leaped on him every night and licked the ointment off his fingers. He spent liberally and received many marks of distinction: the Grand Sharif often accompanied him in the rites of the pilgrimage and invited him to join in a ceremonial washing of the Kaabah, presenting him with a large piece of its covering.

He left Mecca on 2 March 1807 and from Jedda embarked for Yanbu, the port of Medina. He decided to leave most of his servants behind and set off for the second Holy City accompanied by only three attendants, but like Burton after him, he was ambushed on the way. His attackers were Wahhabis who robbed him and turned him back. For fear of being taken for a magician, he destroyed all the specimens of insects and flowers that he had collected and threw away all of his fossils.

He returned to Yanbu and embarked for Egypt which, after running aground again, he reached overland through Sinai. For this dangerous march he had a personal guard of ten Turkish soldiers, supported by fifty more and some armed Arabs. He did not stay long in Cairo, setting out overland for Europe, visiting on the way the Mosque of Omar at Jerusalem: the third holiest building in Islam and then as strictly barred to Christians as Mecca itself. His narrative ends as abruptly as it begins, in Roumania in December 1807.

At no point in his book is there any suggestion that he was not what he seemed, but who was Ali Bey? He was a Catalan named Domingo Badia y Leblich but much remains unclear. He seems to have been born in Barcelona about 1766 and to have studied Arabic and science in Valencia. In 1802 he visited London and appears to have discussed with the African Association the possibility of exploring the continent by going southwards over the Atlas. A year later, as we have seen, he started his travels in an apparently perfect Arab disguise and with immense wealth. It has been suggested that he was working for the Spanish Government but it is more likely that he was working for Napoleon whose interest in the Muslim world is well known.

It was, after all, not much later that the Emperor had soundings taken secretly of possible landing grounds on the Algerian coast, and there is other evidence that he was considering the establishment of European settlements in

North Africa whose grain was needed for his armies.

In 1805 France was again at war with Russia and Napoleon revived his Middle Eastern policy with missions to Turkey and Persia and an attempt to obtain a base at Muscat. It was about this time that Ali Bey left Morocco and moved eastwards. It is quite clear from his own narrative that he did a very detailed survey of the harbours of the Red Sea but this could hardly justify the huge sums that he must have cost his employers: it is tempting to believe that he was an agent in some Great Game which remains as yet undiscovered.

On his return he was received several times by the Emperor and he passed into the service of Joseph Bonaparte. He left Spain when Wellington chased out the French and settled in Paris where he became known as General Badia.

In 1818, after elaborate negotiations with the French Government to secure the financial position of his family, he set out again. His plan was to return to Mecca and then join a caravan of African pilgrims who would be returning home through Ethiopia and Darfur. He hoped

The Kaabah, which Ali Bey was privileged to help maintain. The keys of the 'House of God' are still held by members of the family to which they were entrusted by the Prophet Muhammad.

The two-storey building to the left of the Kaabah is the well of Zemzem, which, according to legend, was opened by the Angel Gabriel to Abraham's slave-girl Hagar and their son Ishmael who were dying of thirst. Burton said that its water tasted of Epsom salts and that he never saw a stranger drink it without a wry face. Pilgrims take bottles of Zemzem water home to their families and friends.

to discover the Sea of Negritia to the east of Timbuktu and emerge in Senegal. However, in August 1818, he died near Damascus apparently of dysentery although French sources suggest that he may have been poisoned by the British Secret Service. It is said that a crucifix was found under his shirt.

It is unlikely that all will ever be known about this mysterious man, but his importance as a traveller cannot be ignored. He made a great contribution to knowledge of two widely separated parts of the Arab world, difficult though it must have been for a man travelling in such state as to be observed of all, to observe much himself.

It would be difficult to think of three men more different than those whose adventures we have attempted to describe in this chapter, for all were typical of their ages. Varthema had the wondering curiosity of a world where much was new and exciting, while Pitts had the belief that all but Puritan Englishmen were scoundrels. In comparison with them, Ali Bey, with his methodical, scientific and linguistic training stands out as a modern man.

Niebuhr and his Companions

KING FREDERICK V of Denmark, who came to the throne in 1746, was a liberal patron of the arts and sciences. He embellished his capital with the beautiful Amalienborg Square, started the Marble Church and founded the Royal Academy of Art, the Botanical Gardens and the Royal Danish Porcelain Factory. These peaceful interests in a continent regularly torn by war encouraged scholars to approach him with hopes of financial support for their pet schemes, for even then academics had to spend much of their time fund-raising. One of the most distinguished professors in Europe was Johann Michaelis of Göttingen: a man of universal learning but whose primary interests were in Semitic studies. He was one of the first to see that understanding of the Bible might be improved by trying to relate the events that it describes to the life and customs of those tribes, both settled and nomadic, which still continued to exist as the Israelites had done.

Recent maps such as that of d'Anville, published in 1755, showed how little was known of Arabia beyond its coasts so in 1756 Michaelis suggested to the King that he would gain great acclaim by sending an expedition to explore the Peninsula. The difficulty, however, was that there was no one qualified to perform such a task and a team had to be selected and then trained. It was not until January 1761 that a party of six men set sail from Copenhagen. They were all young – the eldest thirty-four and the youngest twenty-eight – and they scarcely knew one another.

They carried with them instructions from the King which Michaelis had drafted. They were instructed to stay together and each was to keep a daily diary.

It is possible that Niebuhr himself, wearing robes presented to him in Sanaa by the Imam, was the model for this picture which was published in the first volume of *Voyage en Arabie*, 1776. The incident taking place behind him is probably a clumsy attempt at local colour by the artist.

Particularly they were warned to avoid amorous intrigues with local women and advised that liberties with the fair sex which would have been quite normal in Europe were likely, in Arabia, to lead to savage vengeance. They were all to be equal, they were all to co-operate and none was to try to domineer over the others. Alas, this was to prove a pious hope.

They took also a series of questions from Michaelis which ran to 235 printed pages. There were many linguistic problems based on the Bible. They were particularly told to find out about tides in the Red Sea (a matter of great importance for studying the Israelites' Exodus from Egypt). There were zoological questions on flying fish, basilisks, locusts and desert rats. There were medical questions on elephantiasis, leprosy and the value of circumcision. There were sociological questions about spitting and the proofs of virginity. They were told to report on mermaids, wild honey and the shape of tents. How Michaelis must have enjoyed in anticipation the vast amount of information that he would receive should the expedition prove successful.

The party was chosen to cover all the skills needed in so great an enterprise. There were two Danes; a philologist, von Haven, and a medical man Christian Kramer; two Swedes, Peter Forsskal a naturalist and pupil of the great botanist Linnaeus and Berggren, a tough old soldier who was to be the servant of the group; and two men born in Germany, Georg Wilhelm Baurenfeind, an artist from Nuremberg, and Carsten Niebuhr.

Niebuhr came from a family of poor peasants from the marshes of Friesland and it was not until he reached the age of twenty-two that he really went seriously to school. He had now, at twenty-eight, qualified as a surveyor, and he delighted in mathematics and engineering. He had also learned some Arabic under Michaelis and had been appointed a Lieutenant in the Danish Army. Of all the scientific members of the expedition, he was the least qualified academically, but events were to prove him the most level-headed, the most energetic, and the most durable.

It was eighteen months before the party set foot on

Travelling in Arabia. Following a *wadi* bed, usually dry but occasionally holding a trickle of water, is often the only way to penetrate the mountain regions. This photograph is from the Yemen.

Arabian soil. The first two months there were appalling storms and their ship travelled 2800 miles but got driven back so frequently that they were only thirty miles nearer their goal. We have not space here to record all their various adventures: their horror at the first glimpse of a Turk: their quarrels which were so savage that they accused von Haven of attempting to poison the rest of them: their year in Egypt. During this last period they worked at their various tasks – Forsskal found new plants and was robbed by the Beduins, who, with unaccustomed civility, left him his underpants. Niebuhr surveyed the Rosetta branch of the Nile, produced an accurate map and determined the height of the Pyramids. Von Haven and Niebuhr visited Sinai where the latter became one of the first to copy a long inscription in hieroglyphics.

They left from Suez. Navigation in the Red Sea is always difficult because of coral reefs and fickle currents and the dangers were hardly diminished by their Greek pilot's claim that he could not identify the landmarks unless his eyesight was stimulated with glasses of brandy at frequent intervals. However they reached Jedda without disaster and passed about six months there. Niebuhr as usual noted the things that interested him – he saw people catching ducks by putting seaweed on their heads and swimming up to their quarry and he saw a thief caught by magic. All the suspects were given a piece of paper into their mouths and were told that all but the guilty man could swallow it without difficulty: this proved true.

They could not go inland from Jedda for this would have brought them too near to Mecca. They dubiously embarked in a small Omani boat normally used for carrying coffee which Niebuhr described as resembling a barrel rather than a ship. The Captain dressed in a tiny skirt and the rest of the crew in even less. However, two years almost to the day after leaving Denmark, they arrived at Luhayyah and disembarked in Arabia Felix (present-day Yemen) on 29 December 1762.

They soon felt that the title Arabia the Happy was well deserved for they were made welcome from the very first. The Dola, or Governor, was a former slave but they found in him 'the dignified politeness of a nobleman, the strictest integrity, and the candid benevolence of a true friend of mankind'. If this official was disconcerted at the sudden, uninvited arrival of a group of eccentric professors, he gave no sign and sent them food and offered to pay all their expenses. Their relations with him were always of a pleasant social nature and when they left, they gave him a watch which a man who had been in Egypt undertook to wind for him daily.

Niebuhr was delighted to find 'that the Arabs became ever more courteous the farther we got from Egypt' and he considered the inhabitants of Luhayyah 'curious, intelligent, polished in their manners'. Relations were not even strained when the tactless Forsskal, in order to demonstrate his magnifying glass, asked the Chief of Customs for a live louse: the startled official said that he was not in the habit of carrying such creatures and referred him to a subordinate who fortunately was able to oblige. Forsskal found that he had no longer 'to study plants and robbers simultaneously' and that he could botanise as freely as in Europe. Niebuhr wandered around the villages starting his work on the map of the Yemen which a century later was still the best in existence.

They decided that as, in Niebuhr's words, 'travelling being as little exposed to danger in Yemen as in any country in the world', they would abandon their original plan of going on to Mokha by sea and merely forwarded their heavy baggage which included their specimens. They set off on their donkeys for Bayt al-Faqih which was to be their base for most of March and April 1763.

Niebuhr continued his mapping, hiring a donkey and riding off with its owner as his servant. 'A greatcoat wanting the sleeves, a shirt, linen drawers and a pair of slippers were all the dress that I wore. It being the fashion of the country to wear arms in travelling, I carried a sabre, and two pistols hung by my girdle. A piece of an old carpet was my saddle, and served me likewise for a seat, a table and various other purposes. To cover me at night, I had the linen cloak which the Arabs wrap about their shoulders, to shelter them from the sun and rain. A

bucket of water, an article of indispensable necessity to a traveller in these arid regions, hung by my saddle.' He lived like an Arab for he had learned to content himself with rough bread – practically the only food available along the way. On some of these journeys Baurenfeind came along to draw the countryside and its inhabitants.

Their activities puzzled the local people. Bayt al-Faqih was a centre of the coffee trade and Europeans had been seen there before, but this group was different. They did not appear to be merchants: it was more probable that they were magicians, perhaps makers of gold, for Forsskal was always looking for herbs and Niebuhr making astronomical observations. Once the pair of them were taken for Turkish clergymen and women sought their blessing. The only trouble in this happy period was that most of the party complained of colds or fevers. Not even Kramer, the Doctor, could then have known that Arabia Felix is one of the most malarial places in the world.

At the end of April the travellers moved down to Mokha and there, due to the machinations of a false

above
The ruins of Diriyyah, the old Saudi capital which was destroyed by Ibrahim Pasha in 1818.

above right
The Asir Mountains of the Hejaz, which reach a height of nearly 10,000 feet.

right
The Great Mosque of Sanaa was old when de Varthema visited the city in the sixteenth century. It is believed to have been once a Christian church, rebuilt at the time of the Prophet. Like the Great Mosque of Mecca the one at Sanaa possesses a Kaabah.

friend, they had their first unpleasant experiences in the Yemen. The Customs officers insisted upon opening their specimens and fled before the stench of rotting fish, for the usually impeccable Forsskal had made a mistake in his attempts at preservation. When it became possible to re-enter the Customs, the next articles to greet the officials were bottles of snakes in alcohol. It was clear that the Christians had come to poison all the Muslims and there was uproar: their goods were hurled from the house they had hired and they were ordered to leave the town at once. By a judicious bribe to the Dola, and the help of some resident British merchants, they were permitted to stay. It was in Mokha on 25 May that von Haven died of malaria.

Some days after the funeral, the group set off for Taizz, the largest city of southern Yemen, where, fortunately, the Dola had recently imprisoned a leading merchant and was able to make his house available for his unexpected guests. There they spent a fortnight at their usual pursuits and at enquiring into the local curiosities. Niebuhr heard about the local patron saint – Ismail Mulk – who during his life had been famed for his generosity. After his death a beggar visited his tomb and sought his bounty: an arm

This kind of 'fantasia' is a favourite sport of Arabs, from the Peninsula to Morocco, and a description of a more modern one can be found on pages 160–161. This illustration is from Niebuhr's *Description de l'Arabie*, 1773, and shows one taking place in the Yemen.

emerged from the grave with a letter to the Dola asking that the bearer should be paid 100 crowns. The Governor honoured the 'cheque' but built a barrier around the sepulchre to prevent a repetition. The Dola later showed the same lack of generosity in dealing with the expedition and there were fierce arguments as he tried to order them back to Mokha whereas they were determined to go on to Sanaa.

By now Forsskal was desperately ill and Niebuhr was effectively the leader of the party. They moved northwards and on 11 July Forsskal died in Yarim. Five days later they entered Sanaa, where their reception could hardly have been more hospitable. Shortly after their arrival, they were received in public audience by the Imam. Niebuhr describes how the Prince sat between cushions with his legs crossed in the eastern fashion with his sons and his brothers on either side. He wore a robe of bright green with gold lace on the breast and a great white turban. As the visitors entered, the bystanders all shouted 'God preserve the Imam!' and the potentate graciously presented his hand to be kissed. He made them welcome and later sent them money, sheep and robes of honour.

Niebuhr described Sanaa as a very paradise with its markets full of goods from Europe and India, its magnificent buildings both public and private. The Imam said that the party was welcome to spend a year there at his expense but they were frightened: two of their comrades had died inexplicably and perhaps they felt that the same disease was upon them – if they had died in the Yemen the results of all their efforts would never be known in Europe and the expedition would have been accounted a ghastly failure.

They stayed in Sanaa a mere ten days and then raced for Mokha in the hope of picking up the British ships due to sail for India. It was a nightmare journey for all were horribly ill and part of the way they had to build their own road. They reached Mokha only to find that the boats had left but fortunately another came a fortnight later. Only Niebuhr was able to walk on board: the rest all had to be carried. Baurenfeind and Berggren were dead

The *suq* at Bayt al-Faqih today. It would still be recognizable, 200 years after their visit, to Niebuhr and his friends.

An aerial view of modern Luhayya, the first town in Arabia Felix to be seen by Niebuhr and his companions, 1762.

before they arrived in India. Some months later, in Bombay, Kramer died: though still racked with malaria, Niebuhr was the only survivor.

In December 1764 he set off for home. On the way he visited Persepolis and was the first to give a detailed description of its antiquities, which he thought far more impressive than the Pyramids. He became the first to copy a long inscription in cuneiform and his texts were the earliest pieces of ancient Assyrian to be deciphered. He had made a valuable map of the Gulf by the time he reached Basra in the late summer of 1765.

He went on to Mosul and on the way became the first European to enter the holy city of Najaf where the Prophet's son-in-law Ali is buried. He had made little change in his equipment since his Yemeni days: the only innovation was some brandy in a goat-skin to mix with the often unpleasant water, and a pipe which he had acquired in Persia. On 11 April 1766 a huge caravan assembled outside Mosul consisting of more than 1500 camels carrying silks and the gall-nuts which Europe imported through Aleppo. There were 400 travellers and 150 soldiers to guard them. On 6 June he got to Aleppo and characteristically began research upon various topics there. He stayed in Syria for some time, made the first proper map of Jerusalem and it was a year later before he

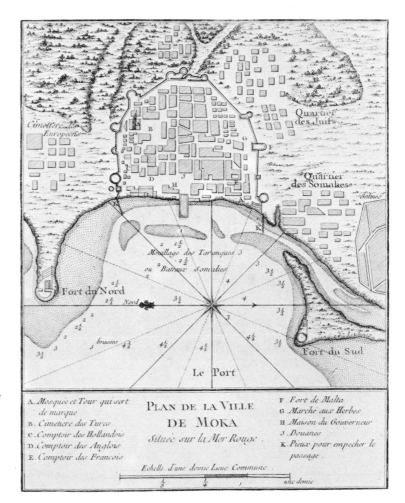

A plan of Mokha about the time of the visit of the Danish party. It will be seen that the British, French and Dutch merchants maintained posts there for the coffee trade. The cemetery where von Haven was buried can be seen outside the town.

left Constantinople on the last stage of his journey. It was November 1767 when he reached Copenhagen. His patron Frederick V was dead and the new King was little interested in the expedition and his indifference was shared both by the learned world and by the general population.

Niebuhr felt himself the sole heir of his colleagues and did his best to publicise all their discoveries. He wrote his own *Description of Arabia* and brought out Forsskal's work with drawings by Baurenfeind. It needs a real effort of imagination to appreciate his achievement for so much of it is today common knowledge. We all know now how Beduins dress and eat, we all agree with him that 'if any people in the world afford in their history an instance of

45

Niebuhr and his party being received by the Imam of the Yemen in July, 1763.

Mokha was once a thriving port, the main exporter of the Arabian coffee trade. Over the centuries the sea has receded and the sands encroach relentlessly on the ruins. The picture shows the Shadili mosque, which in the illustration on page 173 can be seen when it was surrounded by houses.

high antiquity, and of great simplicity, the Arabs surely do. Coming among them, one can hardly help fancying one's self suddenly carried backwards to the ages which succeeded immediately after the flood. We are here tempted to imagine ourselves among the old patriarchs, with whose adventures we have been so amused in our infant days. The language, which has been spoken for times immemorial, and which so nearly resembles that which we have been accustomed to regard as that of the most distant antiquity, completes the illusion which the analogy of manners began'. Again and again reading Niebuhr one says 'I know all this' but one has to remember that he was the first to bring it to the knowledge of Europe. All subsequent travellers have acknowledged their debts to him and only on a few minor

47

points have they shown him to be in error. His account is that of an official and very little personal emerges from it. He was scientifically and philosophically minded, cautious and steady and was hardly the man to masquerade in Mecca or wander with Beduins, but few contributed more

solidly to the study of Arabia.

There is little to say of the rest of Niebuhr's life. Some years after his return he married and eventually settled as clerk to the Council of a remote parish. Later he bought a farm, where he died in 1815 at the age of eighty-two.

Taizz from the north. The town is nearly 4,500 feet above sea-level and the huge mountain behind it, Sabor, rises another 5,000 feet. The city changed little after Niebuhr's visit until it expanded beyond its walls after 1945.

Burckhardt

ONE CANNOT regard Johann Ludwig Burckhardt simply as a traveller in Arabia, for his life's objective was to reach Timbuktu and the source of the Niger. While preparing for this journey he discovered two of what are now the greatest tourist attractions of the Middle East – Petra and Abu Simbel – and spent six months in Mecca, but he never got within 2000 miles of his original objectives.

Johann Ludwig Burckhardt (1784–1817) was one of the most precise and accurate recorders of all the travellers ever to visit Arabia. From an engraving by Richard Westall.

It is not easy to write about Burckhardt in a book such as this. He was a paid, professional explorer who made methodical preparations for his journeys. As a result he had no great adventures and, beyond ill-health, encountered few difficulties. His writings lack any sense of excitement (they are, after all, written in a language not his own) but they are the foundations of all exact knowledge of the areas which he visited. He was tolerant, wise and immensely industrious: a supreme craftsman rather than an artist.

He was born in 1784, the son of a Swiss colonel who had to flee from his native land when it was overrun by the French. Burckhardt studied in Germany before coming to England where he met Sir Joseph Banks, a member of the African Association, which had recently financed several expeditions to the area of the Niger, all of which had ended in the death of the explorers. Burckhardt's offer of his services to attempt to reach Timbuktu with the pilgrim caravans which returned from Mecca was accepted: he was taken on at a guinea a day.

Burckhardt started his preparation by going up to Cambridge in 1808. There he studied Arabic, medicine, astronomy and other sciences. He let his beard grow and started to harden himself by sleeping on the ground, taking long walks and living only on vegetables. The next year he set out for Malta where he assumed the character of an Indian doctor. Asked to demonstrate Hindustani, he gave some sentences in Swiss German and his hearers agreed that it was indeed a barbarous tongue.

Burckhardt spent two years in Aleppo working at his Arabic and proved his mastery by sending back his own translation of *Robinson Crusoe* into that language. He studied Islam equally hard; he had a very great spiritual sympathy with the creed and, indeed, formally accepted it. His knowledge was so great that he was often consulted by local scholars and later no less a person than the Qadi of Mecca pronounced that not merely was he a Muslim, but an extremely learned one. As a by-product, he discovered the first reported Hittite inscription.

During this period he often wandered with the Beduins, particularly with those of the Aneyzeh tribe, and reached as far as Palmyra and the Euphrates. The results of his researches were published and constitute what is really the first ethnographical study of a nomad tribe. Of this time he wrote: 'I have passed among Beduins some of the happiest days of my life; but I have likewise passed among them some of the most irksome and tedious, when I impatiently watched the sun's disk piercing through the tent from its rising to its setting; for I knew that in the evening some songs and a dance would relieve me from my draught-playing companions.'

Curious observations emerge from this period. On how to steal a camel: Burckhardt advises you to seize it by the tail whereupon it gallops off pulling you after it. He describes, also, that while one ostrich sits on the eggs, the partner goes up the nearest hill to keep a lookout but only succeeds in attracting attention. When a hunter approaches, the bird abandons the eggs, whereupon the Arab digs a hole, puts his loaded gun with a long-burning match pointing at the nest and goes away. When all seems clear, the birds return and are shot by remote control. More seriously, he recounted the ceremonies of oath-taking, the duties of hospitality and the concepts of honour: many others have done so since but to Burckhardt goes the honour of being the pioneer.

In February 1812 Burckhardt felt ready to start on the next stage of his journey towards the Niger and moved slowly down through Syria to Cairo which he reached in September. He found, however, that no caravan was expected to set out for West Africa until the following June so he decided to go down the Nile in the chance of finding a route westward from Nubia. If he failed, he hoped to be back in time, but in the meanwhile there was new territory to be surveyed: no European had yet been more than a few miles south of Aswan.

Burckhardt penetrated some 200 miles further south, discovering the half-buried temples of Abu Simbel and having trouble with usually tyrannical and sometimes drunken local Governors. It was clear that he could get neither farther south nor farther west so he crossed the Nile on a rickety craft and retraced his steps. Back in Assiut he learned that there was no immediate chance of going to West Africa, so he decided that he would greatly improve his ultimate chance of doing so by winning the title of *Hajji* – a distinction that would serve as a passport through a largely Muslim area. He therefore joined the caravan which was to take the Nubians and Sudanese to Mecca.

He has left an account of his equipment for this journey. He wore a shirt, cloak and trousers, a skullcap with a cloth around it and sandals. He carried two small notebooks, pencil, penknife, compass, tobacco pouch and flint. For money he had fifty Spanish dollars, and two gold sequins sewn in an amulet; for arms he had a gun, a pistol and an iron-tipped stave. As a further protection he carried letters from the Pasha of Egypt, Muhammad Ali, introducing him as Shaikh Ibrahim bin Abdallah al-Shamy, the Syrian.

For the journey across the desert which was to cover some 1200 miles and last 4 months, he took 40 pounds of flour, 20 of biscuit, 15 of dates, 10 of lentils, 6 of butter, 5 of salt, 3 of rice, 2 of coffee beans, 4 of tobacco, 1 of pepper, some onions and 80 lbs of millet for his donkey. He took also a copper kettle, copper plate, coffee roaster, an earthen mortar to pound the coffee beans, 2 coffee cups, a knife and spoon, a wooden bowl for drinking and

Muhammad Ali, Pasha of Egypt, was originally an Albanian soldier in the Ottoman army. By political genius and ruthless cruelty he made himself master of Egypt for more than forty years. He used his power for rapid industrialization at home and expansionism abroad. In 1811, at the request of his suzerain, the Turkish Sultan, he invaded Arabia to recapture the Holy Places from the Wahhabis. He was helpful and courteous both to Ali Bey and to Burckhardt. Tate Gallery, London.

for filling the water-skins, an axe, 10 yards of rope, needles and thread, a large packing needle, a spare shirt, a comb, a coarse carpet, a cloth for a blanket, some medicines and 3 spare water-skins. For merchandise he took 20 lbs of sugar, 15 of soap, 2 of nutmegs, 12 razors, 2 red caps and several dozen wooden beads. His equipment was to be increased at Shendy by the purchase of a slave for sixteen dollars. Many of his companions were slave-traders.

Burckhardt remained a month at Shendy which he describes in great detail and, in the best Gibbonian manner, goes into Latin for matters which could not be discussed in front of ladies. He could have stayed there forever for the local chief offered him one male and two female slaves if he would accept the post of Royal Gunsmith. On 7 July 1814 Burckhardt and his slave set sail from Suakin on the Red Sea and after a voyage which due to the incompetence of the Captain, lasted nearly a fortnight, managed to reach Jedda in safety.

On arrival in Jedda Burckhardt was taken very ill, possibly with malaria, and thought that he would have died if a local barber had not bled him. Also he found himself penniless for the merchant to whom he presented his letter of credit refused to honour it. With regret he was reduced to selling his slave to whom he had become greatly attached: the price was forty-eight dollars, three times the cost price and almost enough to pay for all the expenses that he had incurred in his desert crossing.

Burckhardt equipped himself as 'a reduced Egyptian gentleman' and wrote to Cairo for funds. At the same time he sent a message to Muhammad Ali who was now at Taif, prosecuting his campaign against the Wahhabis, and soon an order arrived for Burckhardt to be given some money and a new suit of clothes and to proceed to visit the Pasha. Burckhardt had been just over a month in Jedda, including the period of illness and this stay enabled him to write 100 pages of close observation with detailed accounts of trade, customs and even the brands of tobacco available in the *suq*.

In Taif Burckhardt lodged at the house of the Pasha's Armenian doctor, Bosari, whom he had known in Cairo.

The first evening he was received by Muhammad Ali and they chatted of world affairs: the Pasha fearing that the British, who had just overthrown Napoleon, would take advantage of their strength to conquer Egypt. 'A great king,' he declared, 'knows nothing but his sword and his purse; he draws the one to fill the other.' Burckhardt was puzzled by the Pasha's tidings that the Swedes had annexed Genoa: when transliteration problems were sorted out it became clear that it was the Swiss who had taken over Geneva.

Often the Qadi of Mecca was of the party and he discussed theology with Burckhardt who more than held his own: sometimes they prayed together and Burckhardt 'took great care to chant as long a chapter of the Koran as my memory furnished at the moment'. He never knew whether Muhammad Ali doubted the genuineness of his Islam, but religion sat lightly upon the Pasha and most probably he did not care, provided that there was no scandal and he could fix responsibility upon the Qadi. Burckhardt never denied that he was a European but felt

Burckhardt describes the crossing of the Nile in just such a boat – but does not say if a camel was his fellow-passenger, as in this lithograph published in 1822.

that he was suspected of being a British spy and kept under observation. He was determined not to remain in Taif and adopted the expedient of making himself obnoxious to his poor host while saying how comfortable he was and that he proposed to remain for months.

At the urgent request of Bosari, Muhammad Ali gave his assent to Burckhardt's departure. On 8 September 1814 he entered Mecca and apart from a short visit to Jedda to collect some equipment and buy a new slave, he was to remain there until the following January. He wrote, 'During all my journeys in the East, I never enjoyed such perfect ease as at Mecca; and I shall always retain a pleasing recollection of my residence there.' Certainly he did not waste his time: his description covers some 350 pages and a successor as critical as Burton found practically nothing to add or to correct.

He liked the local people, finding them witty, courteous and hospitable. He was amused by their cynicism quoting their saying, 'God has made us great sinners, but He has bestowed upon us, likewise, the virtue of easy

The Red Sea *zaruq* has changed little over the years. This modern example is very much the sort of boat in which Burckhardt would have made the crossing from Suakin to Jedda.

Gezigt der Stad JAMBO van de Z. W. Zyde. ||| *Vûe de la Ville*

Gezigt der Stad DSJIDDA van de Zyde W. t. Z. ||| *Vûe de la Ville de*

repentance,' and that Providence had placed them there to receive alms and not to give them. However, there was one group that he disliked – 'the idlest, most impudent, and vilest individuals of Mecca adopt the profession of guides'. They lay in wait for pilgrims and were reluctant, once they had got their teeth into them, to let them go while they had a penny left. Burckhardt's own guide begged shamelessly, stole his clothes and came frequently to eat with him uninvited, even bringing a bag to take away anything left over. Once he gave a banquet in Burckhardt's honour in Burckhardt's own rooms, invited

Yanbu, the port of Medina, and Jedda, the port of Mecca, drawn in 1762 for Niebuhr's *Voyage en Arabie*. They would hardly have changed in the following hundred years and would have looked much like this to Burckhardt in 1814.

du Côté du S. O.

Côté de l'O. q. S.   C. J. de Stuyser fecit:

all his friends and sent his guest the bill. There was one strange function of these guides: a woman unaccompanied by a husband might not make the pilgrimage and the guides were prepared to offer temporary marriage to wealthy visiting widows. Usually the couple divorced at the end of the season but if the husband refused, the marriage remained valid.

Burckhardt has left an incomparably detailed description of the Great Mosque. He revelled in its beauty during the nights of Ramadan when thousands of lamps glittered in its colonnades and the cool breeze (caused, so said the faithful, by the waving of the wings of 70,000 guardian angels) was a delight after a hot day of fasting. He enjoyed the day-time bustle of the school-children learning their lessons there and noted that the teacher's stick was in constant action.

He performed all the rites of the *haj* and was present at the sermon on Mount Arafat which must be attended by all pilgrims. 'During his sermon, which lasted almost 3 hours, the Qadi was seen constantly to wipe his eyes with a handkerchief; for the law ordains the Khatyb or preacher be moved with feeling and compunction; and adds that whenever tears appear on his face, it is a sign that the Almighty enlightens him, and is ready to listen to his prayers. . . . Some [of the pilgrims], mostly foreigners, were crying loudly and weeping, beating their breasts, and denouncing themselves to be great sinners before the Lord; others (but by far the smaller number) stood in silent reflexion and adoration, with tears in their eyes. Many natives of the Hejaz, and many soldiers of the Turkish army, were meanwhile conversing and joking . . . [and] made violent gesticulations, as if to ridicule the ceremony. Behind, on the hill, I observed several parties of Arabs and soldiers, who were quietly smoking their nargyles; and in a cavern just by sat a common woman, who sold coffee, and whose visitors, by their loud laughter and riotous conduct, often interrupted the fervent devotions of the *hajjis* near them.'

Burckhardt was obliged to remain a month in Mecca after the conclusion of the *haj* because of the unsettled state of the country. Muhammad Ali was still heavily

Ostriches were believed to have vanished from Arabia but only two years ago the drowned body of one was found in Amman. The somewhat complicated method of shooting described by Burckhardt must have been more effective than it sounds! From an Arab manuscript. Biblioteca Ambrosiana, Milan.

engaged in building up his forces to defeat the Wahhabis and had commandeered every available camel to carry his supplies. Once indeed it was rumoured that he had been defeated, and that plundering hordes of Beduins would soon arrive to sack Mecca: Burckhardt and his slave took refuge in the Mosque. However, early in January 1815 the Pasha, leading a cavalry charge in person, overcame the obstinate resistance of the tribesmen (they had gone into battle with their legs chained together so that they could not retreat) and something like security returned to the area.

Burckhardt's camel ride from Mecca to Medina took nearly a fortnight and, like so many of his journeys, was without any incident of importance. Again, like the rest of his marches, it was tiring and uncomfortable for there was no resting place in all the 300 miles. He remained in the city for three months, during eight weeks of which he was so desperately ill that he felt certain that he would die. Conscientious man that he was, he worried less about himself than about all the notes that he had made and which might never reach his employers. His only relaxations were reading the one book that he had with him – the works of Milton – and chatting with his nice old landlady.

His description of Medina inevitably lacks the

comprehensiveness of his picture of Mecca. He was 'struck with the paltry appearance' of the Prophet's tomb and reflected that any minor saint in a Roman Catholic church was better housed. He commented that however strong and fanatical might be the faith of a Muslim, he was not inclined to make pecuniary sacrifices for it.

Medina had even less industry than Mecca and indeed to undertake the simplest repairs to the Mosque it was necessary to bring craftsmen from Egypt: it was not even possible to get one's clothes washed. Its agriculture, however, was highly developed.

Still weak he moved down to Yanbu where he met with the greatest horror of the area – the plague. He was rebuked for heresy for saying so because it was well-known that the Blessed Hejaz had been exempted by Allah from this affliction. Nevertheless people died daily and a camel, richly caparisoned, was led through the streets to pick up all the germs; then it was slaughtered and its flesh left to the vultures and the dogs. His apprehensions were increased when he heard that his slave had piously volunteered to wash the corpses. When after nearly three weeks they embarked in a sambouk, they found that they had the disease on board. On 24 June, Burckhardt re-entered Cairo after an absence of nearly two and a half years.

Burckhardt's health never seems fully to have recovered from all the hardships that he had undergone. Still, however, he yearned for the caravan that was to take him to Timbuktu but found that none was expected in the foreseeable future. He wrote up his travels and spent two months in the Sinai Desert where he came nearer to death at the hands of the Beduins than he had ever done in the Peninsula. He returned to Cairo and there, on 15 October 1817, he died and was buried in a Muslim cemetery. Two months later the first caravan for four years left for Timbuktu.

Burckhardt, like Niebuhr, saw only a small area of Arabia, but it would be difficult to find two men who observed more acutely or recorded more meticulously. His character and his work put him high among the greatest explorers of history.

Burton

OF ALL the characters mentioned in these pages, none was more active in his life nor more prolific with his pen than Richard Francis Burton. No traveller in Arabia – apart from T. E. Lawrence – has attracted more biographies and the first of these was published ten years before his death. A bibliography of Burton's own works runs to more than 300 pages and includes 60 full-length volumes. He wrote on Bayonet Drill, falconry, mining, archaeology, snakes, medicine, engineering, mountain-climbing, religion and sex. He described journeys in every continent except Australasia and on Africa alone he wrote 13 books with a total of over 4600 pages. Arabia remained though, as he said himself, 'the land of my predilection' and it is only with the parts of his life relevant to that area that we can concern ourselves here.

His mother claimed descent from an illegitimate son of Louis XIV and though his father was an army officer, it was often said that the Burtons had gypsy blood. Soon after Richard was born in 1821, his father quixotically threw up his career and went to live a wandering life in France and Italy. His two sons had little formal education except in swordsmanship and half a dozen dialects. Colonel Burton had intended his son for the Church and sent him to Oxford but Richard contrived to get himself expelled and thereby avoided ordination. Even before this he had caused some surprise by challenging to a duel a fellow undergraduate who had sneered at his moustache.

In October 1842 Burton arrived in Bombay as a Second Lieutenant in the service of the East India Company. Soon he showed his incredible skill at learning languages – in

Richard Burton, 1848. He was a master of disguise and possessed an incredible skill at learning languages. Both qualities served him well in Arabia when he arrived there in 1853.

fact one every few months. By the end of his life he knew twenty-nine languages and twelve dialects. He was never content merely to speak the language but always desired to pass for a native. In India he became a master of disguise and would hire a shop and sit, undetected, haggling amongst the merchants. These gifts led to his being ordered by his General to report on the local haunts of vice – an assignment that he found all too interesting and performed all too well. His survey fell into other hands, earned him the name of Ruffian Dick and harmed his career. Other activities did little to improve his reputation: he attempted to abduct a nun and he filled his house with monkeys, one of which he called his 'wife', and sat them at table with him. Official disapproval was so strong that he was denied employment in the second Sikh war of 1848 although he was the only officer who knew the enemy's language. He felt that all roads to advancement in India were blocked to him so he applied for extended sick-leave. He remained for nearly four years in Europe, writing and studying.

In the 1850s people were as interested in geography as they are today in space exploration and it was not too difficult to secure a backer for any well-conceived plan of travel. In the autumn of 1852 Burton offered his services to the Royal Geographical Society 'for the purpose of removing that opprobrium to modern adventure, the huge white blot which in our maps still notes the Eastern and Central Regions of Arabia'. His scheme was to land at Muscat and to go through the Empty Quarter to Mecca and Medina. The Society supported him but his employers, the East India Company, refused to sanction such a journey, maintaining that it was too dangerous. Instead they granted him additional leave to study Arabic 'in lands where the language is best learned'. There would not have been enough time for the methodical expedition that Burton had proposed and he had to reverse his plan and hope to cross from Mecca to Muscat, there to pick up a boat to get him back to India before his furlough expired. In addition to crossing previously unknown parts of the Peninsula, he hoped, as Burckhardt had done, to facilitate further exploration in Muslim lands by

gaining the title of *Hajji* and to help with the perennial problem of the acquisition of horses from Arabia for the army in India.

In April 1853 Burton left Southampton in the character of a Persian nobleman and throughout the voyage he strove to perfect his role in such details as the Muslim way of drinking a glass of water: 'he clutches the tumbler as though it were the throat of a foe . . . ending with a satisfied grunt'. After a month in Egypt he decided to change his character from that of a lord to that of a wandering Dervish and to cease to be Persian – a race disliked and despised throughout Arabia as heretics. Sometime later he assumed his final character, that of a British subject of Afghan origin, educated in Rangoon as a doctor. He bought several changes of clothing, having remarked the importance of always being smart in an area where 'a badly dressed man is a pauper, and a pauper – unless he belongs to an order having the right to be poor – is a scoundrel'. His other purchases included a huge bright yellow umbrella, resembling 'an overgrown marigold', a wooden comb, a goat-skin water bag, a coarse Persian rug 'which besides being couch, acts as chair, table and oratory', a cotton chintz-covered pillow and a sheet. A dagger, a brass inkstand and penholder stuck in

A drawing made by Thomas Shaw in 1808 of a Red Sea urchin. If this were indeed the type of sea urchin that Burton trod on, it is hardly surprising that he suffered severe pains.

his belt, a mighty rosary and some needles and 'a pea-green box with red and yellow flowers, capable of standing falls from a camel twice a day' completed his equipment. His funds for the journey were twenty-five golden sovereigns in a belt under his robes.

Burton had enjoyed the atmosphere of Alexandria: he found there what the Arabs call *Kaif*: 'the savouring of animal existence; the passive enjoyment of mere sense; the pleasant languor, the dreamy tranquillity, the airy castle-building, which in Asia stand in lieu of the vigorous, intensive, passionate life of Europe. It is the result of a lively, impressible, excitable nature, and exquisite sensibility of nerve – a facility for voluptuous-ness unknown to northern regions . . . [where] damp chill air demands perpetual excitement, exercise or change, or adventure, or dissipation, for want of something better. In the East, man requires but rest and shade: upon the bank of a bubbling stream, or under the cool shelter of a perfumed tree, he is perfectly happy, smoking a pipe, or sipping a cup of coffee, or drinking a glass of sherbet, but above all things deranging body and mind as little as possible; the trouble of conversation, the displeasures of memory, and the vanity of thought being most un-pleasant interruptions to his *Kaif*'.

Taking passage on the steamer known as 'Little Asthmatic', Burton arrived at Cairo and took up residence at a native inn or *wakalah*. He practised as a doctor and greatly increased the value of two Abyssinian slave girls by curing them of snoring. More importantly he attended courses in the theological university of El Azhar for, if he reached Mecca, a religious error or a breach of orthodox behaviour would be far more revealing than any linguis-tic faults. There could be many explanations for lack of perfection in language but there could be none for some action that no Muslim would perform. Indeed, it was later persistently rumoured that on his journey between Medina and Mecca, a fellow pilgrim saw Burton perform just such an action and that Burton slit his throat to ensure his silence and his own safety.

Burton provided himself with another £80 for his pilgrimage and set out to acquire a passport. He was scandalised that the Persian Consul, to whom he first applied should demand as much as £4 and reject his offer of £1. His friends, however, introduced him to the Principal of the Afghan College at El Azhar who for a small consideration guaranteed his worthiness to go to Mecca and accompanied him to the Citadel where the necessary piece of paper was produced for the sum of one shilling.

Burton was almost ready to start on his journey when he met another visitor to the *wakalah* – an Albanian officer on leave from the Hejaz, who invited him to his room. Having removed their daggers, the two men proceeded to get extremely drunk. They tried to persuade the other shuddering inhabitants to join them and soused them with cheap brandy when they refused. They called for dancing girls and reeled into a bedroom whence the tongues of two old crones put them to flight. They bellowed insults about Egyptians and the Albanian was just threatening to drink the porter's blood when his servant managed to get him to bed. 'No Welsh undergraduate at Oxford,' wrote Burton, 'under similar circumstances, ever gave more trouble.'

It was hardly surprising that Burton thought it would be as well to leave Cairo as soon as possible. Finding a Sinai Beduin who was travelling the same way, he hired two camels for £1 and set off with an Indian servant for Suez. On the way he met some respectable Medina traders who were returning home and a Meccan lad that he had met in Cairo, Muhammad al-Basyuni. They all joined forces and Muhammad took charge of Burton and all his effects and was to stay with him for the rest of the journey. Burton was little interested in individual characters and his tale lacks the life-like portraits found in Doughty. The nearest that he came to drawing a figure in the round is in his account of this boy Muhammad, mocking staid merchants and solemn Beduins.

At Suez the party took a passage on the fifty-ton *sambook Silk el Zahab* or 'Golden Wire'. As there was accommodation for 60 passengers, the 130 on board began to feel uncomfortably cramped. Burton and his companions, travelling first class almost in luxury were sitting on the poop when suddenly a horde of North Africans

Quba was the spot where the Prophet's camel stopped as he approached Medina after his flight from Mecca. He himself laid the first brick of what was to be the first public place of prayer in Islam, and used to walk out from Medina to pray there every Saturday. The Mosque was rebuilt in Ottoman times, when this fort was also erected to protect worshippers from tribal raiders.

travelling 'steerage' rushed to share their space. There was a savage fight with staves, knives and teeth and the situation was looking dangerous when Burton managed to push down on the heads of the attackers a huge earthen jug full of water. Crushed, and with their ardour dampened, the North Africans solicited peace and respectfully kissed the hands, shoulders and heads of the victors. Apart from running aground, a few more brawls and thrashing the Captain, the passengers reached Yanbu, the port of Medina, without further incident.

Medina, the burial place of the Prophet, as Burton saw, and drew, it in 1853.

When wading ashore at a small port along the way, Burton trod on what was probably a sea-urchin and suffered a badly poisoned toe which was to trouble him for the rest of the journey. This was not an unmitigated disaster for it gave him a pretext for buying a *shugduf*, a camel litter, for two dollars and this made writing notes easier and more private than it would have been on the hump of a camel. For three dollars apiece the party hired camels to take them to Medina – a journey of 130 miles which, with camels travelling at two miles an hour, was to

take eight days. On the way they had to pass through a steep gorge known as the Pilgrims' Pass and there they were ambushed by robbers. Tribesmen swarmed like hornets and kept up a heavy fire. The escort were in great difficulties for the enemy were shooting from behind prepared stoneworks and if one of the Beduins had been killed, the entire population would have joined the battle and overwhelmed the caravan. As it was, the party felt themselves lucky to escape with only twelve men killed.

On 25 July 1853 Burton reached Medina. 'As we looked eastward the sun arose out of the horizon of low hills, blurred and dotted with small tufted trees, which from the morning mists gained a giant stature, and the earth was stained with gold and purple. Before us lay a spacious plain, bounded in front by the undulating ground of Nejd; on the left was a grim barrier of rocks, the celebrated Mount Ohod, with a clump of verdure and a white dome or two nestling at its base. Rightwards, broad streaks of lilac-coloured mists were thick with gathered dew, there pierced and thinned by the morning rays, stretched over the date groves and gardens of Kuba, which stood out in emerald green from the dull tawny surface of the plain.'

Burton on his way to Mecca and Medina.

Burton was to remain in Medina for more than a month and he devoted a whole volume to a description of the city and of the religious rituals in which he took part. He was not impressed by the Prophet's Mosque which he regarded as 'mean and tawdry . . . it suggested the resemblance of a museum of second-rate art, a curiosity shop, full of ornaments that are not accessories, and decorated with pauper splendour'. He was more moved by the great cemetery of El Bakia, which on the Last Day will witness the rising of 100,000 saints with faces like full moons.

On the route from Yanbu, Burton had met a Beduin, one 'Sinful', who would try to help him to go on from Medina to Muscat. However, an argument broke out between two nomads over a camel and blazed into a full-scale tribal war. The sound of firing could be heard in Medina and 'through the streets parties of Beduins, sword and matchlock in hand, or merely carrying quarter staves on their shoulders, might be seen hurrying along, frantic at the chance of missing the fray. The townspeople cursed them privily, expressing a hope that the whole race of vermin might consume itself'. The fighting meant that only the road to Mecca was open. Burton realised that there was little that he could hope to add to Burckhardt's account but was compensated by the chance of being the first European to travel between the Holy Cities by the eastern route.

There was a flurry of preparation – Burton repaired his water skins where the rats had nibbled them – and laid in stocks for a fortnight for himself and Muhammad. He made an agreement to hire two camels for twenty dollars from a Beduin, and his friends advised him to eat with his escort at least once every twenty-four hours so that there should always be some of his salt in their bellies and thus, hopefully, they would be inhibited from treachery. They marched mainly by night, and one stage lasted from 3 pm until 11 am the following morning. Even so there was an ambush and a camel a few yards away from Burton was killed.

On 11 September 1853 Burton reached Mecca where he performed all the rites of the *haj* under the guidance of the boy Muhammad, in whose mother's house he lodged. Muhammad arranged for him to enter the Kaabah and, as a native Meccan in a place where arms were forbidden, was able to kick Persians and Beduins out of the way to enable him to kiss the Black Stone. Burton stoned the Devil as orthodoxy demanded and he attended the great sermon which concludes the Pilgrimage. 'I have seen,' he wrote, 'religious ceremonies of many lands, but never – nowhere aught so solemn, so impressive as this spectacle.' He rode down to Jedda where at the very last moment Muhammad understood that he had been escorting 'a Sahib from India [who] hath laughed at our beards'.

If Burton had returned straight to England he would have been the hero of the hour but instead he decided to stay in Cairo until his leave expired. There he enjoyed himself, still in Arab disguise, by annoying some of his friends who were passing through.

His account of the pilgrimage, like all his books, is a

mass of detailed observation, learned footnotes and wild prejudices, all enlivened with a rather grim humour. He did not add very greatly to the sum of human knowledge but he told the story better and conveyed the atmosphere more excitingly than any of his predecessors. We will pass over his detailed account of religious ritual and pick out odd little nuggets from his story. He noted that cataract is treated by roasting mules' teeth and serving them as a powder and he recounted how the pink-rumped apes of the Hejaz catch birds. They lie face downwards and the birds dive on to what they think an unattached piece of meat: an accomplice monkey who has been hiding nearby pounces on them and wrings their necks.

Burton studied the markets of Medina and found that one could buy fresh ostrich eggs and that an Ethiopian slave-girl might cost more than £20. He took a great interest in the Beduins and remarked how their dancing resembled 'the hopping of bears rather than the inspirations of Terpsichore'. He was the first to comment upon their similarity to Red Indians and it is no surprise to learn that he was one of the founders of what is now the Royal Anthropological Institute. Burton wrote too much and too fast but there is a mine of information in his

As part of the *haj* ceremonies, every pilgrim collects seven stones in the valley of Muzdalifah and hurls them at this representation of the Devil, reciting prayers to confirm his renunciation of evil. The stones are miraculously returned by Angels to the place whence they came. Burton's record of the scene.

works. His encyclopaedic knowledge of the East is shown at its best in his great sixteen-volume translation of the *Arabian Nights* with its massive footnotes. It was a perfect subject for him: Burton was always more interested in vice than in virtue.

It was to be a quarter of a century before Burton returned to Arabia. The story of how he passed the intervening years may be found in his various biographies. Suffice it to say that he was the first European, in 1855, to enter Harar – a feat more dangerous than his journey to Mecca. Later in the same year his camp near Berbera was attacked by Somalis, one of his companions was killed and Burton himself received a spear thrust through the face which caused the scar so prominent in his portraits. In 1858 he and Speke discovered Lake Tanganyika in an attempt to establish the source of the Nile. He visited the Mormons of Salt Lake City and characteristically studied the technique of scalping.

In January 1861 Burton married the pious and aristocratic Isabel Arundell, who, upon first catching sight of him ten years before, had told her sister, 'That man will marry me.' She helped him to obtain Consular Posts in West Africa, Brazil, Damascus and finally Trieste. During

The ceremony remains the same, though the method of recording it may differ. A modern photograph of the Stoning of the Devil.

much of this time her duty was 'Pay, Pack and Follow' as he moved around the world, but she was the most devoted of wives and wrote the most adoring of biographies.

Bored in Trieste and seeking for something to do, Burton remembered that one of his old friends of the Cairo *wakalah* had recounted that on his way back from the Pilgrimage, he had found a rock containing gold. This had taken place in the most northerly part of the Arabian Peninsula which is separated from Sinai by the Gulf of Aqaba – the old Land of Midian whose prowling hosts had been routed by Gideon some 3000 years before. Burton had been interested in gold as far back as his Indian days and he knew something about mining from all his travels: Ismail, the Khedive of Egypt, had practically ruined his country by his extravagance and was desperate for new resources. Financing such an expedition as Burton suggested was just such a gamble as might save his position.

Burton tracked down his old friend, now aged eighty-two, and persuaded him to accompany the expedition despite the fact that he was expecting the birth of his fifth child. They were accompanied by a French mining engineer and a military escort and sailed from Suez at the end of March 1877. Burton regarded the enterprise as a continuation of his journey to the Holy Places.

The party spent three weeks in the area and Burton returned with the conviction that gold could be mined farther inland. They found an exciting-looking substance which upon tasting turned out to be camel droppings of immense antiquity; they found ancient inscriptions, some new plants and insects but they did not find any gold. This did not, however, prevent Burton from telegraphing to the Khedive that the expedition had been a complete success as they returned to Cairo with their samples of stone, gravel and sand.

Burton had no difficulty in writing a book even about such a limited exploration. Full of his usual learned footnotes and references, it breathed a great spirit of optimism. Fortunately the Khedive also remained hopeful and fitted out a much larger party. Four Europeans, 6

Egyptian officers, 32 Egyptian soldiers (mostly emancipated negroes), 30 quarrymen, a Greek cook and waiter and a carpenter disembarked in Midian on 19 December 1877.

The group was immensely active. Burton estimated that in 4 months it covered 2500 miles and brought back 25 tons of samples. It surveyed the site of 18 ancient settlements but once again it did not bring back any gold. Geographers say, however, that Burton's survey of the area was his greatest contribution to the knowledge of Arabia, far more important than his first more spectacular journey.

There was a brief suggestion that Burton might go to the Sudan and work under Gordon but, wisely, he saw that they were a pair unlikely to work together in harness. There was a brief visit to survey the possibility of gold-mining in the Kong Mountains of West Africa, but Burton's active life was slowing down. Increasingly he devoted himself to literary activities – the *Arabian Nights* and what was to have been his masterpiece, a translation of *The Scented Garden* with footnotes containing the distillation of all his knowledge and experience. In 1886, considerably to his surprise, he was knighted. In October 1890 he died. Lady Burton took two steps to preserve his memory: she built an extraordinary tomb in the shape of a Beduin tent in Mortlake Cemetery and, deeming them obscene, she burned all the manuscripts to which he had devoted his last years.

It has often been written that Burton was an Elizabethan born out of time, but it would be truer to say that he would never have been a conventional citizen of any age. He was too wild, too undisciplined, too self-willed: he had, as he said of himself, 'every talent except that of using his talents'. He was often right: he was one of the first to argue that malaria was spread by mosquitoes and he was just as often wrong: he thought Negroes incapable of advancement. Perhaps, after all, the Victorian age with all its opportunities was the best one for him, but the final word should rest with his younger friend Swinburne. 'Burton,' he wrote, was 'one who found not on earth his kin.'

Palgrave

WILLIAM GIFFORD PALGRAVE was born in 1826, the son of a most distinguished scholar who played a leading part in the establishment of the Public Record Office. Sir Francis Palgrave had been born Francis Cohen but had assumed his wife's maiden name upon marriage. All of his sons achieved distinction: Frank as Professor of Poetry at Oxford and compiler of the famous *Golden Treasury* once found in every household, Inglis as Editor of the *Economist*, and Reggie as the successor of Erskine May as Clerk of the House of Commons.

The future traveller, known in the family as Giffy, had a successful career at Charterhouse and at Oxford before joining the Bombay Infantry. He caught his first sight of Arabs on the way to India when he crossed Egypt in January 1848. He had scarcely been away a year when he astounded his family with the announcement that he had resigned his commission and joined the Jesuit order; later he was to say that this was due to an overwhelming desire to work as a missionary amongst the Arabs. He remained in India in the novitiate until the summer of 1853 when he was sent to Rome to begin training for the priesthood. He was not in fact ordained until March 1857, by which time he had been in the mission field of Beirut for nearly two years.

His first task was to perfect his Arabic, in which he became so proficient that he could refer to it as almost his mother tongue. He preached eloquent sermons, wrote hymns and taught in that language in the schools that he had helped to found. These were, however, extremely turbulent years in the Lebanon, years of peasant revolt, of religious strife between Christians, Muslims and Druzes.

William Gifford Palgrave (1826–88), soldier, Jesuit, secret agent and finally diplomat whose account of his Arabian travels still causes controversy.

Turkish Governors, European Consuls, missionary orders all intrigued and fished in the troubled waters. Palgrave, on secret missions to the Druzes and to the descendants of the medieval Assassins, entered with enthusiasm into all that was going on. There were rumours that he had preached as a Druze leader: certainly he did undercover work amongst the Orthodox.

In the summer of 1860 there started a series of massacres as the Druzes slaughtered their Christian neighbours. Palgrave, with his army background, was asked to take military command of his flock but regretfully declined. He was, indeed, lucky to escape with his life from a savage mob in Sidon. His superiors recalled him to Europe to report and to attempt to raise money to help those that had survived to start life again. He gave a series of lectures, and was received by the Pope and, more importantly, by Napoleon III.

The Emperor was always deeply interested in the Muslim world. He supported his wife's cousin, Ferdinand de Lesseps in his construction of the Suez Canal, he twice visited Algeria where he proclaimed himself King of the Arabs and he sent troops to Syria to protect the Christians there. He may, indeed, have entertained a truly Napoleonic vision of two Arab Empires – one East and one West of Suez under the tutelage of France. An early step in this scheme was to tempt the Viceroy of Egypt, still under Turkish sovereignty, to declare himself independent under the suzerainty of France.

Palgrave was Napoleon's chosen agent in this plan, and his qualifications were impressive, for he combined linguistic skills (later he learned Japanese in two months) with military and diplomatic experience. He failed to win over the Egyptian Viceroy but in February 1862 he set off for Arabia on a mission the scope of which is still obscure. No one in Europe had any recent information about events in Nejd – indeed no Western traveller had been there since Sadlier's rapid visit more than forty years before. He managed to convince his somewhat dubious religious superiors that he might succeed in converting the Wahhabis.

Palgrave was generally known in Syria as Father

A desert inn on the overland route to India. A picture published in 1847, the year of Palgrave's journey.

Michel Cohen or as Father Michel Sohail, but for the purpose of this journey he became Saleem Abou Mahmood el-'Eys, a travelling quack doctor and pedlar. His chosen companion was a young Greek schoolmaster from the Lebanese town of Zahleh who looked like an Arab and spoke the language like a native. His name was Geraigeri but he was to travel under the name of Barakat, describing himself according to need as his master's brother-in-law, associate merchant or assistant quack. They took with them medicine sufficient to 'kill or cure half the sick men of Arabia', some learned treatises in Arabic to impress people and some more practical ones in English kept carefully hidden. For commerce they took cloth, glass necklaces, pipe-bowls and coffee. They were dressed in stout blouses of Egyptian hemp, loose cotton drawers and red leather boots.

In the preface to his book Palgrave was to say that his motive was 'The hope of doing something towards the permanent social good of these wide regions; the desire of bringing the stagnant waters of Eastern life into contact with the quickening stream of European progress; perhaps a natural curiosity to know the yet unknown,

Palgrave remarked that such a sandstorm differed from Hell only in that it was not eternal. From a lithograph of 1821.

and the restlessness of enterprise not rare in Englishmen.' He also wrote of the need to know more of areas 'of whom future destinies we seem likely to be in no small measure, under Providence, the arbitrators'.

The two disguised men set out from Maan (in present-day Jordan) on 16 June 1862. They were accompanied by three Beduins, two of whom he described as 'utter barbarians in appearance no less than in character, wild, fickle, reckless and the capacity of whose intellect was as scanty as its cultivation'. Unlike most travellers, Palgrave has little good to say of the nomads whom he regarded as treacherous, promiscuous brigands and 'not a true sample of the Arab race . . . only a degenerate branch of that great tree, not the root or main stock'. On the other hand he was equally unusual in praising the pleasant courtesy and kindness of the town-dwellers who were to treat Doughty so roughly.

The stories of Palgrave and Doughty are so contrasting that they seem to be describing different worlds. We shall come later to Doughty's account of the sufferings and indignities that he underwent but Palgrave said, 'A Christian and an Englishman may well traverse Arabia, and even Nejd, without being ever obliged to compromise either his religion or his honour: but for this, perfect acquaintance with Eastern customs and with at least one Eastern language, together with much circumspection and guardedness in word and deed, are undeniably required.' Most people, he said, regarded Christianity as a sect of Islam and it does not seem that Palgrave went out of his way to correct them. He gives the impression that he attended prayers in mosques on more than one occasion.

With this discretion, Palgrave's travels seem rarely to have been dangerous. They were, of course, uncomfortable with sandstorms and a summer heat that led him to remark that Hell could hardly have been different apart from its eternity. There were pleasant interludes as in the prosperous oases of Jawf where he disposed of much of his merchandise. The people were hospitable and offered him a business partnership – and indeed a wife – if he cared to remain.

However, he tore himself away and went on to Hail, where he was kindly received by the Emir, Talal ibn Rashid, who even walked through the town hand in hand with him. This reception was particularly reassuring for there had been an awkward moment when Palgrave encountered someone who had known him in Damascus as a European and possibly even as a priest. A second man also recognised him but again Palgrave was fortunate in being able to bluff his way out.

Palgrave was impressed by Talal and he wrote, 'Among all rulers and governors, European or Asiatic, with whose acquaintance I have ever chanced to be honoured, I know of few equal in the true art of government to Talal.' He paints a picture of an efficient yet tolerant régime, almost an ideal state, encouraging trade and regarding attendance at the mosque as a mere exhibition of good manners towards one's neighbours. Talal sent his sons to the two 'doctors' to show his confidence, although he realised that there was an ulterior motive for their visit. He thought that they had come to buy some of his incomparable horses but finally they asked him for a private interview and told him everything. He heard them attentively and warned them to be discreet, adding, 'Were what now passes between us to be known at large, it might be as much as your lives are worth, and perhaps mine also.'

On 8 September 1862 the two travellers left Hail. They were furnished with a passport signed by Talal – and carried a heavily sealed letter from his uncle to deliver to Abdallah ibn Faysal ibn Saud, the eldest son of the Imam and the acting ruler of the Wahhabi state. In it was written that the bearers were practitioners of magic (a capital crime) and added significantly 'God forbid that we should hear of any evil having befallen you.' Palgrave commented that he still had the letter when he left Riyadh: implying that he knew the contents and had realised he was carrying a death warrant.

Palgrave and Barakat entered Riyadh under the guidance of one of the few characters who really comes alive in his book – the failed carpet-seller Aboo-'Eysa who now earned a precarious living looking after Persian pilgrims. They made friends with some of the highest officials whom they treated as patients and whose hospitality exemplified the old Nejdi proverb that a guest in a house is its master. It was not long before Palgrave was received by Prince Abdallah whom he described as looking like Henry VIII and having many of the same characteristics – pride, cruelty, courage and political skill. The Imam Faysal was old and tired and Palgrave, like others in Riyadh, anticipated that when he died there would be a struggle for the succession between Abdallah and his much more attractive younger brother Saud, whom Palgrave described as having 'the bearing of a hussar officer'.

Abdallah determined not to await events but to be the first to strike. Several times he casually hinted to Palgrave that he could find a use for some strychnine and finally asked directly for some, saying that he would brook no refusal. Palgrave hissed in his ear, 'I have no mind to be an accomplice to your crimes, nor to answer before God's judgment-seat for what you will have to answer for. You shall *never* have it.' 'His face became literally black and swelled with rage; I never saw so perfect a demon before or after. A moment he hesitated in silence, then mastered himself, and suddenly changing voice and tone began to talk gaily about indifferent subjects.'

It was now the end of November 1862 and Palgrave had completed his researches into Wahhabi history and politics and was anxious to leave. He was about to do so when a messenger from Abdallah arrived in the middle of the night telling him to come at once. Abdallah motioned him to sit near him and there followed a prolonged silence broken suddenly by the Prince's saying, 'I now know perfectly well what you are; you are no doctors, you are Christians, spies, and revolutionaries come hither to ruin our religion and state on behalf of those who sent you. The penalty for such as you is death, that you know, and I am determined to inflict it without delay.' Palgrave, whose account of the incident is the only one that exists, looked his accuser coolly in the face, admitted to being a Christian, denied being a spy and defied him to put them to death: 'You cannot, and you dare not.' He had, he pointed out, been his guest and that of the king, his father, for more than a month. Firmly he told the baffled tyrant 'to leave off this nonsense' but Abdallah had one more card to play. At his command a slave came in, bearing a single cup of coffee which he presented to Palgrave. The challenge was obvious: was it just a cup of coffee? Refusal would give Abdallah, an Arab to whom the laws of hospitality were sacred, a reason to take offence. Palgrave drank it and asked for another.

The reception room of the Emir of Jabal Shammar. Starting as provincial Governors this family, the head of which was always known as Ibn Rashid, dominated north-eastern Arabia for a quarter of a century, despite its internal feuds. Eight of the first ten Emirs met violent deaths—usually at the hand of relatives. This picture dates from a decade after Palgrave.

'Abdallah's face announced defeat.' Palgrave made a little sociable conversation before calmly leaving the room: a classic case of British steadfastness and phlegm face to face with a native despot.

Even so, he decided to slip unobserved out of Riyadh. Aboo-'Eysa laid a trail of deception behind them and they reached Hufuf without trouble. There they stayed for some time before going down to the Gulf which he accurately described as 'like a leaden sheet, half ooze and half sedge'. There Barakat left him and returned home, eventually to be ordained and to become Patriarch of the Melchites. Palgrave decided to continue his travels, accompanied now by Aboo-'Eysa's servant and he visited Bahrain, Qatar and the Trucial States. Off Sib the Arab vessel was wrecked and though Palgrave, by taking charge when the Captain lost his nerve, saved some of the crew, he lost all his notes and was washed ashore totally penniless. The Sultan received the survivors kindly, gave them money and eventually Palgrave reached England safely by way of Baghdad and Aleppo.

In the spring of 1865 his *Narrative of a year's journey through Central and Eastern Arabia* was published with a dedication to Niebuhr whose 'intelligence and courage' had first opened Arabia to Europeans and had inspired the writer. In an obituary after Palgrave's death *The Times* was to refer to it as 'one of the most interesting and romantic books of travel that have ever delighted the public'. But that is a view which today is difficult to

The market place of Hufuf, the town where Palgrave rested after his dramatic adventures in Riyadh.

The Bedouin does not merely ride the camel – he has been described as the parasite of his beast. He drinks its milk, eats its meat, and uses its hair to weave clothes and tents. He also employs it as a unit of account (damages for death or injury may be reckoned in camels).

accept for Palgrave's narrative seems to embody many of the worst faults of Victorian writing. Quotations and allusions are dragged in for no apparent reason but to show the author's wide culture: what, for example, can one make of his descriptions of the writings of Muhammad ibn Abd al-Wahhab as 'Treatises which a Supralapsarian might peruse with edification, and an Antinomian almost mistake for the Acts of the Synod of Dort'? Again there is the now insufferable archness which led men of his age to say 'nether limbs' when they meant legs. Palgrave once refers to 'a certain saltatory insect very common in southern Europe and in Syria ("letters four do form its name")' when he meant a flea. If the present writer may intrude a personal note: of all the authors read for this book only Palgrave, despite some vivid passages, was found irritating and pompous.

There is, however, a more serious charge that has been levelled against Palgrave. It has already been hinted that his account of his interview with Abdallah may be less than accurate and his tale has numerous internal inconsistencies and passages that are manifestly incorrect. He saw mountain ranges which subsequent travellers did not, and he apparently did not notice the only lake in Arabia, in the Aflaj region south of Riyadh. No one who has been to both places could possibly think that Qatar has twice the population of Bahrain and a subsequent explorer found his plan of Hufuf so wildly inaccurate that he could not even orientate it. One may also wonder why, if indeed he were shipwrecked off Muscat, he did not approach the resident British official.

Of all Palgrave's critics Philby, who covered all the same ground, is the most categoric. He doubts whether Palgrave even reached as far as Hail and he is convinced that the rest of his story is pure fiction. Against this it must be said that Doughty and Blunt accepted his tale as completely accurate while T. E. Lawrence was of the opinion that 'He was in the Philby-Thomas class as an explorer and wrote brilliantly.' We shall probably never be able to establish the facts with certainty and perhaps the best solution is to accept the verdict of Hogarth that Palgrave undoubtedly made most of the journey that he described but that to him 'a story was a work of art not to be spoiled in the telling for lack of a little embroidery'. Palgrave was less interested in solid facts than in conveying impressions and in this, right or wrong, he usually succeeded.

Palgrave was never to return to Arabia. He did a report for Napoleon including a plan for linking Syria to Egypt under French domination. He had hopes of renewed employment in the Arab missions but when these were frustrated, he left the Jesuits and the Catholic Church. The rest of his career is beyond the scope of this book but his travels were by no means ended. He was appointed Consul in Eastern Anatolia where he served from 1866 to 1873. He married and had three sons. He continued his consular career with posts in the West Indies and the Philippines until 1878 when there was a possibility of his returning to the Middle East as assistant to General Gordon. Instead he went to Bangkok, and his final post was Montevideo where, as British Minister, he died in October 1888. His body was brought home and he is buried in Fulham.

Doughty

CHARLES MONTAGU DOUGHTY was born in Suffolk in August 1843 into a landed family traditionally connected with the Navy and the Church. He went up to Cambridge where he studied geology, and, as an undergraduate, explored glaciers in Norway. While still in his early twenties, he decided that the vocation of his life should be to serve his native language 'the old manly English, full of pith and stomach'. This he always regarded as a duty and a privilege, for late in his life he wrote that 'it is the prerogative of every lover of his Country, to use the instrument of his thought, which is the Mother-tongue, with propriety and distinction; to keep that reverently clean and bright, which lies at the root of his mental life . . . putting away all impotent and disloyal vility of speech, which is no uncertain token of a people's decadence.'

Doughty, serene but alert, in old age. From the portrait by Eric Kennington, 1921. National Portrait Gallery, London.

He spent some years preparing himself for this task, studying Dutch, Danish and other languages to increase his understanding of his own. He spent a year in Oxford reading medieval and Elizabethan poets and, above all, Chaucer and Spenser. Then he wandered forth in quest of a theme – a story that he could tell in the style that he was fashioning. He passed through Spain and Italy where he witnessed an eruption of Vesuvius in 1872 and noted 'the whissing of the writhen slags'. He went on to Greece and to Cairo whence early in 1875 he rode across Sinai to Petra, where he heard of a city reputed yet more wondrous – Madain Salih, near the northern border of the Hejaz.

Madain Salih, the cities of the Prophet Salih, was famous in Muslim mythology: seven great cities cut out of the rock had grown rich and luxurious as a result of their position on the great incense route from South Arabia to Memphis and Jerusalem. The Prophet Salih had summoned them to repent, but, scoffing, the people had demanded a sign and he provided one: a pregnant camel stepped out of the mountainside. The crowd, however, slew the mother and the hills opened up to swallow the calf whose groans, it is said, can be heard to this day. Their impiety was punished by a whirlwind which destroyed their houses, turning them upside down. Both Burckhardt and Burton had failed to reach these ruins and Doughty determined to see them, despite the refusal of the Ottoman authorities, still controlling most of the Arab east, to let him go.

Friends, however, said that no Pasha could prevent his joining the caravan setting out for Mecca as long as he did not venture into the forbidden Hejaz. He clothed himself, therefore, as 'a Syrian of the middle sort of fortune' and attached himself to a group of Persians with whom he felt that he would be less conspicuous. He took with him about £13 in gold, two small notebooks, a sextant, an aneroid barometer, a thermometer, a cavalry carbine and a revolver concealed underneath his shirt. He took also a medicine chest for he proposed to pass as a doctor and to earn money by vaccinations. He carried also two scientific treatises in Arabic and a copy of Chaucer: little enough luggage but still enormous by the standards of the Beduins with whom he was to wander. The caravan consisted of perhaps 6000 pilgrims, with a guard of 300 infantrymen, 200 cavalry, 2 guns and 100 Ageyl – wild tribesfolk little better than bandits. Doughty, now known as Khalil (a name borne by people of all religions in Syria) was warned by his companions, 'Woe to the hajjy that fainting or lingering falls into the hands of the Ageyl! Ouff! they will cut his purse and his wezand' (throat).

The attractions of the pilgrim caravan to a lover of Chaucer are obvious and Doughty revels in describing the dogs that walk the 2000 miles from Damascus to Medina and back, the slaves that carried the charcoal for the pipe-smokers and the white cock which accompanied the Persians. He narrated that when a Persian lady died en

route, her servant slaughtered a camel and sewed her body within the raw hide so as to carry it into the Holy Land. Marches were long – sometimes twenty-four hours out of twenty-six – and halts were brief and then 'there is a short struggle of making ready, a calling and running with lanterns, a confused roaring and ruckling of camels, and the tents are taken up over our heads'.

Towards the end of November 1876, Khalil arrived at Madain Salih. The Pasha leading the *haj* – a corrupt rascal who 'licked fat from all beards' – had recognised him as a Christian and so gave him in to the charge of a Moroccan who commanded a little fort built over a well. This *kella* was to be his base until the caravan returned from Mecca. He wandered around copying inscriptions and drawings from the tombs cut in the rocks. He was never in danger except from sudden outbursts of fury from his guardian 'snatching my beard with canine rage, the ruffian plucked me hither and thither, which is a most vile outrage'. It was, however, only the first of many that were to befall him in the following eighteen months.

Doughty never tells us about his motives and gives no real reason for his decision not to return to Damascus with the *hajjis*. Undeterred by a friendly warning 'Mark well

Mount Sinai, and the road into Arabia, from a lithograph published in 1839. Doughty made his way to Petra through Sinai.

Doughty's description of the pilgrimage from Damascus conveys the same atmosphere as this eighteenth-century picture. The one he joined in 1876 was made up of some 6,000 people.

the hostile and necessitous life of the Beduw! Is it to such wild wretches thou wilt another day trust thy life? See in what matter they hope to live – by devouring one another! It is not hard for them to march without drinking, and they eat by the way, only, if they find aught,' he joined a little tribal group. Its chief was Zeyd, 'hollow his cheeks, his eyes looked austerely, from the lawless land of famine, where his most nourishment was to drink coffee from the morning, and tobacco; and where the chiefest Beduin virtue, is *es-subor,* a courageous forbearing and abiding of hunger', in whose constant quarrels with his wife Khalil had to mediate. Despite this poor advertisement for matrimony, Zeyd offered to find Doughty a wife if he would join them for good.

Apart from occasional clashes with the avaricious Zeyd, Doughty seems to have enjoyed this period – 'a pleasure it is to listen to the cheerful musing Beduin talk, a lesson in the travellers' school of mere humanity' but he found their music less attractive 'the Beduin singer draws forth stern and horrid sounds from his rabeyby or viól of one bass string, and delivers his mind, braying forcedly in the nose'. He watched women seething asses' dung in a pot to serve with milk to the sick. He was present when raiders

87

carried off many of the tribal camels: no one seemed very concerned and the remainder were shared out among the losers. They wandered into Teyma – once mentioned in Genesis – where he found the people 'slippery merchants, and swimming in all looseness of carnal living'.

By now it was April and 'the wilderness fainted before the sunny drought . . . we seemed to breathe flames. All day I gasped and hardly remained alive, since I was breathless and could not eat'. Doughty decided that he had had enough and returned to Madain Salih, determined to travel down to the coast to take passage in a dhow to Egypt. After a day in which he was constantly insulted and refused water and a night in which he overheard people discussing whether to kill him, he decided that he could not survive the heat of the coastal plains: he had to turn back to the cooler uplands.

From the end of May he wandered for four months in the Harra area, 'an iron desolation; what uncouth blackness and lifeless cumber of volcanic matter! – a hard-set face of nature without a smile for ever, a wilderness of burning and rusty horror of unformed matter'. There was one unpleasant incident when a tribesman accused Doughty of abandoning him in the wilderness but was reproved by a committee of shaikhs, and a moment of danger when a raiding party was reported to be near: 'Mount, Khalil and prevent them' – The women added, "And that quickly, we would not have thee slain." The children cried, "Ride fast from them, uncle Khalil".' This shows the pleasant relationship that Doughty enjoyed with the nomad women who liked to ask him such questions as to whether there were female Christians and whether the moon might be seen in Western lands.

In October Doughty entered Hail in Jabal Shammar, now ruled by Muhammad ibn Rashid of whom the Beduins said 'he has committed crimes which before were not known in the world'. Doughty saw his rise to power as a medieval saga of murder and witchcraft but this formidable potentate received him at first with courtesy. Indeed he was offered a high position if he would become a Muslim. The people, however, were extremely hostile to the Christian who adamantly refused to pretend to be anything else and they regarded his presence in their midst as an insult to their religion. Twice he was assaulted and once he was robbed and the Emir had to keep intervening to protect his uninvited guest. Finally the Emir gave him a letter of safe conduct and bade him be gone. It was almost a year to the day since he had entered Arabia.

Doughty's destination was Khaybar – a town famous in history for it had been the site of a large Jewish community which had stoutly resisted an attack led by the Prophet Muhammad in person. It was famous also for its dates and for its fevers; 'how strange are these dank Khaybar valleys in the waterless Arabia! A heavy presentiment of evil lay upon my heart as we rode in this deadly drowned atmosphere'.

Doughty was fortunate to reach Khaybar alive. Ibn Rashid had sent with him three low caste and unwilling Arabs who, when opportunity offered, deserted him. However, for once Doughty was discreet and did not noise abroad that he was a Christian. Some Beduins took pity on him and he found a man who would conduct him to his destination.

Khaybar was under direct Turkish administration and Doughty thought that he would be unmolested there: perhaps he might have been if he had not immediately told the Governor that he was a Christian. As so often he refused to compromise, glorying in his integrity and little regarding the trouble to which he was putting all around him. The poor illiterate Negro who represented the majesty of Turkey had no idea what to do when his embarrassing guest refused to leave so he took Doughty's money 'into safe keeping' and gathered up the rest of his papers and sent them to his superior, the Pasha of Medina. Doughty was to remain there some six weeks, not ill treated but constantly insulted by the Governor who, on more than one occasion, struck him but was restrained by public opinion from anything too violent.

During this period Doughty made what proved to be his best friend in Arabia. 'Uncle' Muhammad al-Najumy was a retired soldier and he and Doughty gardened together, gossiping as they worked. Najumy told Doughty of military expeditions after which pairs of ears from the enemy dead were salted and sent to Medina. Doughty narrated something far more improbable to his auditor: 'I told the good man how, for a fox-brush, shaikhs in my beled [country] use to ride furiously in red mantles, upon horses . . . with an hundred yelling curs scouring before them; and leaping walls and dykes and all in adventure.' When finally 'the world, and death, and the inhumanity of religions parted us for ever', Najumy refused any reward saying 'only this I desire of thee that thou sometimes say "The Lord remember him for good"'. It is sad to learn that Philby, visiting the area seventy years later, heard that Najumy had been murdered while quietly enjoying a game of draughts.

The Pasha of Medina was sympathetic to Doughty, but as an official could not tolerate his presence in the Holy Land. He returned the papers and ordered the Governor to send him back to Hail. Doughty refused to go until all his money had been restored. And when he did it was not a pleasant march; once he and his companions were so thirsty that they thankfully drank water full of wriggling white vermin, and at another time Doughty and his fellow travellers came to blows.

Doughty re-entered Hail on 1 April 1878 and found it almost deserted – Ibn Rashid was away on campaign. Deprived of that prince's protection, he was the victim of fanatical attacks: once indeed it appeared that someone was bringing a knife to circumcise him by force. They offered him money to change his religion and he replied: '"Though ye gave me this castle . . . the pits and sacks of hoarded silver which ye say to be therein, I could not change my faith." "Akhs, – Akhs – Akhs – Akhs!" was uttered from a multitude of throats: I had contemned, in one breath, the right way in religion and the heaped riches of this world! and with horrid outcries they detested the anti-christ.' He cannot have had too much regret at being told to leave the town at once.

He was put in the charge of the two companions who had brought him from Khaybar. They had no wish for his presence and he stumbled after them over burning gravel.

One of the tombs of the ruined cities of Madain Salih, the first goal of Doughty in his travels in Arabia. In ancient days the cities enjoyed great prosperity from their position on the incense route to Memphis and Jerusalem.

Suffering from opthalmia he could hardly keep them in sight and he felt that his heart might burst: blood spurted from his nose. Finally they abandoned him, to some unfriendly company. His hosts were ready to murder him but a Beduin woman intervened on his behalf. Eventually he found guides to take him south-east to Buraydah – where they warned him on no account to say that he was a Christian, for no non-Muslim had ever entered the town. Unluckily he was in a public place when the muezzin gave the call to prayer and the fact that he did not go to the mosque was obvious to all. When challenged he refused, as always, to deny his religion.

A daily sight for Doughty—an old gentleman holding his camel stick and resting on a camel saddle, prepared to talk for as long as any one would listen. From Julius Euting, *Tagbuch Einer Reise in Inner-Arabien*, 1896.

A small crowd collected and Doughty was assaulted, stripped and robbed of all his possessions. The Emir restored them but demanded that his troublesome visitor should leave the town. He allowed him one day to see the surprisingly prosperous city but during the afternoon a crowd gathered to demand his blood. There were only two women in the house and boldly they denied the presence of a stranger, crying 'Ha! uncivil people; who be they that throw up stones into the apartment of the hareem? . . . O ye devil-sick and shameless young men!' The return of his host dispersed the mob.

A guide was appointed to take him on to Unayzah, a short distance south, but abandoned him on the outskirts. Doughty was now completely alone and almost penniless. No one was responsible for his safety but by now he well understood Arab customs so he begged some foul water from a gardener and thus established the bond of hospitality between them. His host later sent him on to the Emir of the town, Zamil.

Zamil was kindly and hospitable and so were many of the leading citizens, for it was a trading community and its members were used to strangers. However the Emir's uncle stirred up some fanatics who stoned Doughty's dwelling, stole his watch and reduced his total wealth to less than £1. The Emir felt obliged to order his departure but made no difficulty in acceeding to his friends' suggestion that he might be recalled. It was not safe for him to enter the town but he lived for six weeks in a garden outside and received many visitors. On 5 July

1878 he set out on what was to be his last Arabian journey.

His friends at Unayzah had arranged for him to accompany a caravan taking tons of butter down to the Hejaz. They provided him with a camel on which he trailed slowly after his companions, tormented now by an ulcer. He had been bitten by a dog and reflected as he rode 'Ah! what a horror, to die like a rabid hound in a hostile land.' However, he came nearer to death for a different reason: a mad Sharif demanded his conversion to Islam and 'with wild cries he bid me rehearse the *shahud* or die upon his knife'. Then 'more bystanders gathered from the shadowing places: some of them cried out "Let us hack him in morsels, the cursed one."' He was robbed of his pistol which he had preserved but never used in all his vicissitudes and it is possible that his adventures would have ended there but for the fortunate arrival of an old Negro servitor of the Grand Sharif who insisted upon escorting him to his master's palace at Taif. The Sharif received him kindly, entertained him while he recovered his health and then sent him to Jedda and safety. On 3 August 1878 he entered the British Consulate.

It was ten years before *Arabia Deserta* appeared – 'the seeing of an hungry man and the telling of a most weary man'. Doughty was adamant that the material was less important than the manner of its telling and that he preferred, despite the advice of an editor that it should be rewritten by a competent literary man, to leave it unpublished rather than to change a word. The result is that he produced what T. E. Lawrence called 'a book not like other books, but something particular, a bible of its kind'.

Doughty did not add much to the geographical knowledge of Arabia but the picture that he painted is unique. He never tried, as did so many writers, to see the Beduins from outside, as leading an ideal life of freedom and romance. Rather, as if from the inside looking out, he showed the harshness and difficulty of their lot. He saw their occasional respites, their hospitality, and their delight in a rare good meal and in a rest in the shade. He caught the nuances of their society, their mixture of greed and generosity, of reckless courage and cowardice, of courtesy and churlishness. He saw how it was dangerous to be the first to reveal one's identity, and was amused how his host always asked where he had spent the previous night and what he had eaten; determined if possible to provide better fare. Where else but in Arabia could a man live for eighteen months with practically no money and never actually starve?

The well at Teyma, the *Tema* of the Old Testament. Tema was one of the sons of Ishmael, and gave his name to the town.

Equally with the Beduins, Arabia itself is the hero of the book. He captured – and it is no coincidence that he was a geologist – the incredible monotony of 'the sered wasteful wilderness, full of fear, where every man's hand is ready against other, a lean wild grit and dust, stiffened with everlasting drought', under 'a perpetual grey more than blue heaven'. For the traveller, he wrote, 'here is a dead land, whence, if he die not, he shall bring home nothing but a perpetual weariness in his bones'.

No explorer, probably, ever suffered more indignities and hardships than Doughty. Indeed 'I passed one good day in Arabia: and all the rest were evil because of the people's fanaticism.' However he was himself hardly less fanatical 'a bankrupt of Fortune, yet I must prefer death to any false barbarous acknowledgement of Muhammad, whose bastard Arabian faction in religion is the most dangerous grown confederacy and secret conspiracy surely, in the whole world'. Burton acidly criticised him for bringing all his sufferings upon his own head by his obduracy and unwillingness to make the slightest concession, but, nevertheless, he remains an heroic figure. Lawrence says that even forty years later, the Arabs remembered him as such in places where his travels were still discussed. There is something strange yet splendid in remaining an English gentleman, serious, courteous, trustful, in the Beduin encampments of the Arabian desert. However unwillingly, he himself stands out with the Beduin and Arabia as the third hero of his book.

The story of the rest of his life is briefly told. He married after his return from Arabia (the Beduin thought that he had hired out his wife during his travels) and became almost a recluse. He devoted himself to poems which he hopefully regarded as 'a continuation · of

Chaucer and of Spenser, such as conceivably they might have written in the present'. *The Dawn in Britain* is immensely long, about three times the length of *Paradise Lost* while in other poems he foretold the coming of war and of space-travel. He was kindly and generous to those who followed in his footsteps, despite the fact that he seems to have lost interest in Arabia. He died in Sissinghurst in January 1926 and is buried in Golders Green.

I have tried, as far as possible, to tell Doughty's story in his own words, but to gain a real impression of his style – of his mixture of ancient Saxon words with early Victorian English and Arabic, it is necessary to quote him at length. This is a representative passage: to understand it, it is necessary to know that a *menzil* is a camping-ground, *beyt* is a dwelling and *ghannem* a flock. Doughty is writing of the dogs that accompany a tribe. 'At the alighting, the booth-cloth is hardly raised, when (if suffered – this is the sheep-keeper tribes) they creep into the shadow and scrabble the hot sand, and dig with their paws under them, to make their lair upon the cool soil beneath. A dog strayed at the menzil, and running by strange tents, is hooted – *ahl-ak, ahl-ak* "to thy household, sirra!". The loud nomad dogs, worrying about the heels of all strange comers, are a sort of police of the nomad encampment. A few of them are perilous snatchers with their teeth; a man may come by, skirmishing with his camel-stick behind him, and the people call off their dogs. But if there be only hareem at home, which do but look on with a feminine malice, a stranger must beat them off with stone-casts. Some woman may then cry "Oh! oh! wherefore dost thou stone our dog?" And he "The accursed would have eaten me." – "But, O thou! cast not at him" – "Then call him in thou foolish woman and that quickly, or with this block now, I may happen to kill him" – "Eigh me! do not so, this eats the wolf, he watches for the enemy, he is the guard of our beyt and the ghannem; I pray thee, no not another stone." – "Mad woman, before he eat me I will break every bone in his skin, and cursed be thy tongue! with less breath thou canst call him off!"'

Philby

PHILBY'S GRAVE in Beirut bears the inscription 'Greatest of Arabian explorers' and, in very many ways, this claim by his son is justified. None of the writers that we have discussed saw so much of the Peninsula, visited as he did practically every corner of it nor traversed it so many times in so many different ways. None of them spent more than twenty months in Arabia: Philby was there for most of forty years.

Philby during the very active years of the 1930s.

Harry St John Bridger Philby (generally called Jack or Shaikh Abdallah) was born in Ceylon in 1885 and used cheerfully to suggest that he was not really himself but a local baby mistakenly picked up by a careless nurse. After a very successful career at Westminster and Trinity College, Cambridge, he joined the Indian Civil Service and arrived in Bombay in December 1908. When, some two years later, he married, his best man was his cousin, the future Field-Marshal Montgomery. Philby acquired the reputation of being a difficult colleague – indeed he claimed to have been the first Socialist in the Service – but he made his mark as an exceptional linguist and a first-class administrator.

In November 1914, after the declaration of war on Turkey, British and Indian troops landed in Iraq and soon overran the province of Basra. The Turks removed what government records had existed and there was a frantic need for efficient organisers. Philby was among those selected and arrived for his first experience of life in an Arab country in November 1915. He was saddled with a multitude of tasks, from collecting revenue to editing a propaganda newspaper.

In November 1917 Philby had the experience which

changed his life. The Arab Revolt had broken out in June of the previous year, and the British were anxious to prevent the old rivalry between the Sharif of Mecca and Ibn Saud, ruler of Nejd, from hindering the efforts of the former against the Turks, and, if possible, to enlist the latter under the Allied banner. There had been no official contact with Ibn Saud for more than two years and Philby was ordered to find out his current views. In the best traditions of the Indian Empire, he landed at Uqayr, near Bahrain, in a solar topee, breeches and spurs. At his very first stop, his hosts demanded that he should make himself less conspicuous by wearing local dress, for he was to travel through a land of religious zealots, whose souls, he was told, 'are sour with fanaticism' and who had no wish to see their country polluted by the presence of a Christian.

After seven days on camel-back Philby reached Riyadh and for the first time met Ibn Saud. Abd al-Aziz ibn Abd al-Rahman ibn Saud, to give him his full name, was the greatest figure that the Peninsula had produced for more than 1000 years – heroic warrior, decisive ruler and eloquent poet, towering a head taller than his followers. His charm was as overwhelming as his stature for he was witty, generous and hospitable. He could not have had a more perfect background than his vast mud palace, with its retinue of soldiers and slaves – or a desert tent under a starlit sky. It is too strong to say that Philby fell in love with him but he came for all time under the spell of the monarch and of the civilisation that he represented. In return Ibn Saud appreciated Philby's devotion, and valued his knowledge. Almost at once the visitor was admitted into the intimacy of the royal family, playing with the young princes and sitting regularly as a member of the group of boon companions with whom the king liked to relax.

The original plan was that Philby's arrival should coincide with that of an emissary from Cairo who would come overland from Jedda. This was frustrated by the Sharif, who alleged that Ibn Saud had so little control over his tribes that such a journey would be impossible. Mischievously, Philby, with the enthusiastic support of

Although Palgrave described the
waters of the Gulf as a 'leaden
sheet' they take on beautiful
colours at sunset. Kuwait, 1961.

Ibn Saud, decided to prove this untrue by travelling across to Jedda himself. With careful timing he informed his superiors in such a way that there was no opportunity for them to forbid it. Ibn Saud provided him with camels and an escort and the party rode the 450 miles to Taif in fifteen days. It was not an easy journey, for his companions hated the task of guarding an infidel and some were unwilling to defile themselves by eating with him. Villagers along the way were equally unwelcoming. When he reached Jedda he had completed the third crossing of the Peninsula in a century.

After political tasks in Jedda, Cairo and Jerusalem Philby was back with Ibn Saud in the spring of 1918 on a new mission: this time it was his task to persuade him to attack Ibn Rashid whose territory lay between the battlefields of Palestine and Mesopotamia. Ibn Saud was very susceptible to pressure from the British for he was almost entirely dependent upon their financial support. The subsidy of £5000 a month that they gave him

A crowd assembling outside Ibn Saud's palace in Riyadh to celebrate a religious festival.

Ibn Saud in 1933.

represented a substantial part of his income. On one occasion he told Philby that the total contents of his Treasury were £3000 and $4000 and another time Philby quotes him as roaring at one of his followers, who grumbled at his receiving an infidel, 'see, thou dog, see these clothes I wear, nay, the very food I eat – all these I have from the English; how darest thou then abuse them?' Philby, therefore, did not have too much difficulty in persuading Ibn Saud to undertake the campaign but could not prevail upon him to allow him to accompany it, for Ibn Saud could not afford to be seen attacking fellow Muslims at the instigation of Christians. As a consolation, however, he provided him with an escort for a fifty-day journey to the previously unmapped Wadi Dawasir, some 500 miles south of Riyadh. Philby brought back valuable scientific and cartographic information and a burning determination to be the first to cross the Empty Quarter.

Upon his return Philby found that the war was practically over and that official policy had changed: indeed it was now desired to maintain Ibn Rashid as a barrier between British-ruled Iraq and the possible dangers of Saudi expansion. He was therefore recalled to his official career in Baghdad and was soon plunged into hot disputes about the future government of the country. It was at this period that he was overheard to make a memorable remark to a colleague at a noisy party: 'I didn't hear what you said – but I entirely disagree.' No wonder that his Chief sighed that Philby was always convinced that anything from a constitution to a fountain pen had been put together on fundamentally wrong principles. In July 1921 he and his masters had a rare moment of unanimity: both sides agreed that he should leave. He went off on holiday to Persia and took advantage of being able to travel with the correspondent of *The Times* to reveal the most embarassing secrets of the Iraq administration.

Philby was perhaps fortunate to be given another chance of Government employment. In November 1921 he arrived in Amman to succeed T. E. Lawrence as Chief British Representative to the newly formed and, indeed,

practically non-existent Emirate of Transjordan. It was a lawless period and another British officer describes how he saw a man chasing another with a drawn sword. He was laughingly commenting upon strange native sports when the pursuer caught up with his quarry and struck off his head in the middle of the market. Philby had enjoyable moments but in two years he had quarrelled irretrievably with both the local ruler and his own chiefs, so by the middle of 1924 he was unemployed.

During these Transjordan days, Philby had met the famous travel-writer Rosita Forbes. Still in her twenties, she had already made a name for herself by romantic exploits described in still more romantic books. In heavy disguise she had visited the Libyan oasis of Kufra where only one European had preceded her. Lord Northcliffe

Great areas of Arabia are covered by black lava. Doughty spent days crossing country like this on foot in scorching heat.

A striking rock formation east of Riyadh. The sandy desert stretches away to the horizon.

102

The house in Jedda where Philby lived for many years. It has now been destroyed and replaced by a modern construction. The people in the foreground are clearly pilgrims in their *ihram*.

offered her £5000 to go to Mecca, but according to her tale, at the very last moment she felt that she could not in conscience masquerade as a Muslim. Her next book described how she had quelled mutinies on a dhow in the Red Sea en route to explore an unknown part of south-west Arabia. Scarcely drawing breath, she was off to Morocco to write the autobiography of a celebrated bandit. The *Daily Telegraph* offered her £4000 to cross the Empty Quarter in company with Philby, who would provide the solid scientific work while she attended to the glamour and the publicity. None of the governments of the areas concerned were to be told in advance and, to avert suspicion, Philby and Rosita arranged to proceed independently to Nejd. She and a cine-photographer set off for the Gulf while Philby headed for Jedda.

The old quarrel between the Sharif and Ibn Saud had flared into open war and, after capturing Mecca, the king's armies were besieging Jedda. With his usual self-confidence Philby offered to mediate – and was told sharply by the British government to mind his own business, under pain of losing his pension rights. Furthermore, he was forbidden to enter the interior. He and Rosita met in Aden but again their project was vetoed. Rosita wept on the Resident's desk and departed with her photographer to explore Abyssinia. She vanishes from our story for we cannot here recount her adventures with Balkan Queens and amorous Latin Americans – to say nothing of Ataturk, Stalin, Hitler and Mussolini. Philby returned forlornly to London.

A year later, having raised some financial support Philby formed a small trading company in Jedda which was to be his base for most of the rest of his life. He imported cars and arranged for the trains of camels to pull them over the sand-dunes. He had a hand too in the introduction of telephones and wireless sets although it took the personal prestige of Ibn Saud to convince the more conservative elements that the distant voice that they heard was not that of the Devil in person. Above all he took particular pleasure in helping to ensure that the concession to prospect for oil went not to a British company but to the Americans for he regarded them as

The harbour and city of
Mukalla, the Hadhramaut port
on the Indian Ocean. Mukalla
was the point reached by Philby
on the first crossing of Arabia
from north to south.

A striking photograph by Philby of a force of Ibn Saud's men, 1918.

Philby and his escort riding into Jedda, December 1917, at the end of the first of his many crossings of the Arabian Peninsula.

Philby recorded this on one of his journeys: water is sometimes so scarce that it is impossible to let the camels drink and water is poured up their nostrils from a kettle.

freer from the taint of imperialism. Ironically he did not realise until too late that these actions were to change out of all recognition the old austere Arabia that had so fired his imagination.

He resumed his friendship with Ibn Saud and strengthened it by becoming a Muslim in August 1930. At least when abroad he does not seem to have taken very seriously the prohibition of alcohol. His relations with the British authorities were almost uniformly bad; we may quote a report of 1937 after his return from the Hadhramaut: 'Philby was in his most heroic Prometheus mood . . . to his desire to bring the light of science to mankind, is now added a quite ferocious intention to expose the alleged duplicity of HMG towards the Arabs of the Peninsula.' They were not much worried about his possible influence over Ibn Saud for they regarded the latter as by far the more level-headed. Meanwhile the French watched enviously what they regarded as one more triumph for the dreaded British Secret Service in getting its man into a position from which he could direct the policy of a nation and intrigue against long-suffering France.

At the end of 1931, although cruelly disappointed that Bertram Thomas had forestalled him in crossing the Empty Quarter, Philby resumed his Arabian exploration. He set off from Hufuf with an escort of fourteen men provided by Ibn Saud, thirty-two camels (all female except for one gelding) and provisions for three months. Although as travellers they would have been exempt, the party decided to keep the Ramadan fast until evening when the Beduins would wash out their mouths with camel's urine. When the camels' feet were slashed to pieces by stones, strong men held them down and sewed strips of motor tyre across the cuts.

As usual he quarrelled with his companions, for they wanted to adopt the normal Arab habit of travelling by night to avoid the heat while he, of course, intended to see and map the country. They wished to make detours only for the sake of hunting oryx while he insisted on doing so to visit things they regarded as of little interest. When he had difficulty in getting his way, he embarrassed them by refusing to eat or drink. Angrily they shouted at him, 'we toil for you in vain; we strain the camels till they break – all in vain. You are ever displeased and critical.' He would reply 'as for the heat in my heart, maybe God put it there when he created me, but it is you folk that enflame it with your contrariness'. He had hoped to continue south to the Indian Ocean but his escort swore that this was impossible – they did not know the way, the tribes were hostile and the whole party would perish. He learned later that after one particularly savage argument they discussed the possibility of killing him as he slept and were only deterred by the fear that they might not all be able to hold to the same story under interrogation.

Finally he agreed to turn back – 'The Empty Quarter had routed us. . . . At last sleep blotted out the nightmare of the day ... perhaps the most terrible of all my experience'. It is hardly surprising that he should write that 'the physical exertion of desert travel is as nothing compared with the nervous strain'. He and his men turned westward and covered 375 miles in ten days across the completely waterless desert. The camels were refreshed only with an occasional kettle of water poured into their nostrils while Philby himself went for 250 miles without drinking. The whole march was 1700 miles achieved in ninety days, and for three months of really strenuous work, his men received an average of £10.

After this great camel ride, most of his later exploration was done by vehicle. On one journey his wife accompanied him and became the first European woman to cross Arabia from sea to sea. From his accounts and those of people who went with him we can see the modern explorer in action. He used a tent only when it was raining and he wore the same garments until they dropped off. His chief luggage was his mapping apparatus and the rest of his kit included skinning knives, a butterfly net, a lamp to attract moths, killing bottles and boxes for specimens. Invariably he took a radio and there would be occasional halts to listen to commentaries upon a current Test Match, while, with luck, the evening might produce a concert of Gilbert and Sullivan. He always carried a packet of *The Times*, never opening more than

Pilgrims from overseas arrive in Jedda, the port of Mecca, and prepare for the overland journey to the Holy City.

110

one a day. The final relaxation before sleep was the Crossword Puzzle at which he claims never to have cheated.

He took copious notes on all his journeys and his written-output was enormous, tremendously thorough and accurate. His flat, matter-of-fact style prevents his books from being read as literature but they are a quarry of information. He told a friend of the present writer that his method was to put in 'everything' and as he was an ornithologist, zoologist, geologist, ethnologist, historian, archaeologist and topographer, 'everything' means what it says. The works were then garnished with Latin tags, dredged from his classical education. Only occasionally were there whispers of mistakes – caused, perhaps by his guides, fearing his legendary temper, preferring to invent a name rather than admit to ignorance and risk a drubbing.

It was his use of modern transport, added to the active support, sometimes financial, of the king, that enabled Philby to see so much more of Arabia than any of his predecessors. In May 1936 Ibn Saud asked him to map his boundary with the Yemen, so Philby made his way to the ancient settlement of Najran where he made archaeological discoveries of the greatest importance – including a

Philby's picture of his first visit to Mecca shows how the Great Mosque was surrounded by houses.

script never before found in southern Arabia. With his usual disregard for diplomatic niceties, Philby decided to press on into disputed territory, towards an even more fabled site: his target was Shabwa, one of the cities claimed as the capital of ancient Sheba and, as far as he knew, never visited by a European. It was an appalling journey over the sand-dunes and one night he was stuck as a sand-storm raged. 'For sheer physical discomfort,' he wrote, 'the experience of my life cannot match it.'

He reached his goal, although later he found that he had been preceded by Hans Helfritz. A guard of honour greeted him, and in reverse of usual drill, marched past him. The writer has experienced this form of Arab greeting and is surprised that they did not fire their rifles as they went, for that is the practice of the area: the nearer a bullet goes to the head of the honoured guest, the greater the compliment intended. As Philby had Saudi soldiers with him, the people of Shabwa assumed that he had come to annex them to Ibn Saud's realm and the British authorities in Aden shared the same suspicion. Murmuring about obtaining a replacement for a broken axle, Philby travelled slowly down to the coast at Mukalla where he was greeted by a telegram telling him not to wait upon the order of his going. He chuckled that he had achieved the first crossing from North to South and that he had tweaked the nose of the imperialist by so doing – 'I could wish for no better reward than the impotent rage of Aden.' As usual results were contrary to his expectations. The British, alarmed by the revelation of a threat from the north, started to adopt a forward policy in the Hadhramaut and new areas were brought under effective control. On his way home he entered the Yemen to have a peep at the ancient city of Marib. The Imam was no more amused than the British had been.

Early in 1939 Philby returned to England and plunged into politics both international and domestic. He tried to solve the problems of Palestine by suggesting that the Arabs should allow the Jews to have the country, except for a 'Vatican City' of Jerusalem in return for £20 million and unity under Ibn Saud. He stood for Parliament as a pacifist and lost his deposit. In December 1939 he returned to Arabia and announced to all who would listen that the British would lose the war and richly deserved to do so for opposing Hitler whom he regarded as a mystic, the equal of Christ and Muhammad. The next summer he told Ibn Saud that he wished to go to India and America to conduct anti-British propaganda. He crossed Arabia again and took ship to Karachi where he was arrested and returned to England for detention under the Defence of the Realm Act. Although he was released after a few months, no one wished for his services, even during the greatest crises of the war.

With the peace, Philby returned to Arabia to resume his business activities and to live with a pack of baboons and a sixteen-year-old slave girl in his houses in Jedda, Mecca and Riyadh. He continued his exploration and became increasingly interested in archaeology: it is largely due to him that the number of inscriptions in the ancient Thamudic script of North Arabia increased from 2000 to 13,000. He recorded the belief that these people had left a cave full of fabulous treasures guarded by scorpions the size of oxen. Other Beduin opinions to be found in his works are that locusts come out of the nostrils of fish and that thunder is caused by angels beating gongs to precipitate rain on places chosen by God.

Although he prospered from the new wealth of the country, Philby, like king Ibn Saud, felt increasingly out of sympathy and bewildered by the changes that it brought about. After the death of his old friend in November 1953, Philby became bitingly critical of the waste and corruption that he saw about him. In April 1955 he went into what was for him exile in the Lebanon, pursued by invective denouncing him as a Zionist and an imperialist spy. A little over a year later he returned in vehicles provided by the Saudi government. He continued in active business and scholarship, making frequent visits to Europe. It was on his way back from an Orientalist Congress in Moscow that he died, in Beirut in September 1960.

Philby's first days in Arabia were in a country that was still the land of Niebuhr and Doughty: his last in a country with television, an airline and the fastest growing national income in the world. The age of exploration had ended. With the aid of aerial photography, all Arabia had been mapped and the areas unvisited by Europeans on the ground were mere creeks and backwaters. No one contributed more to the knowledge of the Peninsula than this figure so thoroughly English despite his Islam and his constant opposition to Whitehall. He made his own rules, went his own way always convinced that he was right. He might have been a typical Victorian individualist if, within his bosom, there had not lurked the demon of pure cussedness.

A photograph of Philby taken in 1946, which gives a very good impression of his character.

Travellers in the Hejaz

THE HEJAZ is the Holy Land of Islam, the land where the Prophet Muhammad received his revelation. Most visitors who approach it through the port of Jedda would agree with T. E. Lawrence when he wrote how 'the white town hung between the blazing sky and its reflection in the mirage which swept and rolled over the wide lagoon, then the heat of Arabia came out like a drawn sword and struck us speechless'. He went on, 'the atmosphere was oppressive, deadly. There seemed no life in it. It was not burning hot, but held a moisture and sense of great age, and exhaustion such as seemed to belong to no other place. . . . One would say that for years Jedda had not been swept through by a firm breeze.' However he did enjoy its architecture which looked 'as though cut out of cardboard for a romantic stage-setting' – Elizabethan half-timber work gone mad with its extraordinary balconies on which the ladies could take the air, seeing without being seen. Lawrence did not describe the unique feature of the city – the tomb of Eve, Mother of Mankind, which was a white-washed building with a dome marking her navel. She must have been a lady of rather unusual stature for Burton calculated that she had apparently measured 120 paces from her head to her waist and a further 80 down to her feet but that she had been a mere 6 paces broad.

Just over forty miles inland, past guarded check-points through which no non-Muslim may pass, set in a barren valley, lies Mecca. The life of the city centres around the Great Mosque which covers an area of more than 8 acres. There are 7 minarets and 17 gates, always open, pierce the walls against which stand houses. In the middle, directly under the Throne of Heaven and above the core of the seven earths, stands the Kaabah – the House which originally God ordered His angels to build before man was created and which was reconstructed by Abraham. In its south-east corner, mounted in a circle of silver and worn by the kisses of generations of pilgrims, is set the Black Stone given by Gabriel to Abraham. The Kaabah, which is draped in a rich silken covering worked with pious texts in gold thread, is a cube above 40 feet high without windows but with a single silver-plated door some 7 feet above the ground. The keys of the House are still kept by the same family to which they were confided by the Prophet and it is opened by them on special occasions. Nearby stands a two-roomed structure which covers the well of Zemzem which, legend says, saved Abraham's slave Hagar when she and her son Ishmael were dying of thirst.

In the neighbourhood is the uninhabited village of Mina where, it is believed, Abraham prepared to kill his son at the command of God and where, to commemorate this sacrifice, the Faithful slaughter sheep on the most solemn festival of Islam. Close at hand are the stone pillars which represent the Devil and at which the pilgrims, as a symbol of their rejection of evil, hurl stones. A little further away is Mount Arafat, where tradition has it that Adam and Eve met again after their expulsion from Heaven and where the Prophet preached his farewell sermon.

Nearly 300 miles north lies Medina where there is a mosque of the same pattern as that of Mecca, and which stands where the Prophet's camel halted after the flight from his enemies which is regarded as the inauguration of the Islamic era. In one corner of the enclosure can be seen the room where Muhammad died and where he lies buried with his immediate successors and where a vacant sepulchre awaits the greatest Prophet of earlier times, Jesus the Son of Mary. A grill surrounds the Chamber and a dark green silk curtain prevents pilgrims from seeing the actual tombs. It is a simple place and bears no resemblance to the fantastic tale told in the Middle Ages, which reported that the coffin of Muhammad hovered above the earth through the cunning use of magnets.

Medina was to have been the scene of the first incursion of Christians into the Holy Land. In the 1180s, Renaud de Chatillon, in theory a Crusading hero but in practice a robber baron, planned to grab the wealth which legend had accumulated around the tomb. His men landed on the Red Sea coast and penetrated to within a day's march of the city before they were overwhelmed by superior forces. It is said that the survivors of the battle were tied on to camels with their faces to the animals' tails and taken to Mina where they were put to death.

As we have already said, Ludovico de Varthema who reached Mecca in 1503 was the first European to give a description of the city. He was, however, by no means the first Christian there although it is difficult to be precise about earlier visitors. In 1497 the Milanese Ambassador in London reported to Duke Ludovico Sforza that he had met a certain John Cabot, 'a man of kindly wit and a most expert mariner'. This old salt boasted that by sailing westward out of Bristol he had discovered an island off the coast of Asia which he had called Newfoundland and annexed in the name of Henry VII: this almost convinced

Old Jedda. The picturesque buildings have largely been replaced in the last few years.

the Ambassador that the world was round. Before this exploit Cabot claimed that his interest in the spice trade had taken him many times to Mecca where caravans arrived from all over Asia.

It seems most probable that several Portuguese, during their great age of expansion reached Mecca and Medina. About 1500, a captain Gregorio da Quadra was ship-wrecked and imprisoned in a cistern at Zabid by the king of Yemen – 'an ill conditioned fellow'. During eight years of captivity he learnt the language so well that he could pass as an Arab and he earned his living by making skullcaps (presumably of the sort that people still use today as the basis of their turbans). A revolution overthrew his persecutor and the new king took him in his entourage to the Holy Cities. In Medina he was, however, so overcome by religious emotion that he shrieked aloud, 'O Prophet of Satan, if thou art the one whom these dogs adore, manifest to them that I am a Christian, for I hope that by our Lord's mercy, that I shall yet behold this, the house of abomination, become a Church for His praise, like is that of Our Lady of Conception in Lisbon.' His hearers, astonished by this outburst, were convinced that he must be a saint and vied with one another to invite him to lunch. However he rushed off on foot for Basra and became the first European to cross the fearful sand desert of the Nafud. He lived off locusts and became so blistered by the sun that he could no longer bear to lie down. To sleep he dug a pit deep enough for him to stand erect and it was in this pitiful state that he was rescued by a passing caravan. He ended his days as a Capuchin Friar.

One of the next accounts of Mecca to reach the West is to be found in *The World Surveyed or the famous voyages and travailes of Vincent Le Blanc or White of Marseilles who from the Age of Fourteen years to Threescore and Eighteen, Travelled through most parts of the World. The whole work enriched with Many Authentick Histories* which appeared in English in 1660. As one of the 'Authentick Histories' is that of a Prince who was transformed by a wicked step-mother into 'an exceeding pretty and tractable Ape' we may perhaps venture to think that we have in Le Blanc the true compatriot of Tartarin de Tarascon. Certainly the reason that he gives for his continual travelling is credible – to escape from his wife, 'one of the most terrible women in the world' and so is the tale of the Arab who, feigning madness, hurled 'an abundance of vermine' over his friend's shirt and then stole it when the victim removed it for washing. But it is also odd that no one else has ever noticed the very large number of bulls in the Mosque at Mecca which Le Blanc asserts were kept there to draw the water from Zemzem.

In 1643 Mecca received a surprising visitor – a Catholic Bishop. Mateo de Castro, the son of converted Brahmins, was born in Goa and ordained in Rome. Upon his return he quarrelled with his colleagues and decided to plead his case before the Pope in person. Why he went via Mecca, how he managed to do so and what he thought of it must remain tantalizing mysteries.

During the last years of the eighteenth century British ships began to pass regularly through the Red Sea, avoiding the Cape route by linking with others calling in Egypt's Mediterranean ports. Their arrival, often by accident, at the ports of the Holy Land caused alarm and Eyles Irwin who was on the first ship to enter Yanbu found himself imprisoned by a nervous Governor. 'We warned him not to offer any insult the British flag which the most barbarous natives had been taught to respect' but he insisted upon detaining them until instructions came from his master, the Sharif of Mecca. Most writers complained of the incredible heat but few solved the problem more ingeniously than the famous journalist James Silk Buckingham, who made the voyage in a net hanging over the side of a dhow, by means of which he could immerse himself in the water when he so wished.

It is told in an earlier chapter how Ali Bey, in 1807, and Burckhardt, in 1814, visited Mecca but between these years a Russian citizen, Ulrich Jasper Seetzen, reached the Holy City. He had been called the best qualified explorer ever to visit Arabia for he was a superb linguist and had a wide knowledge of practically every form of science. In 1802, with financial support from the Czar, he set out for the east where he spent seven years, often wandering as a beggar, before feeling confident enough to venture on the pilgrimage: his object was perhaps to win the title of *Hajji* which would be of use to him working for the Russian Intelligence in Africa or Muslim Central Asia. Seetzen succeeded after some difficulties which included a stiff *viva voce* examination on religious topics. Then, in the guise of a doctor, Hajji Musa, Seetzen went to Yemen, planning to cross the Peninsula to Muscat on his way to Basra and Central Asia. His large train of camels attracted cupidity and his mineralogical and botanical researches aroused suspicion that he was a magician or had secrets of buried treasure. Late in 1810 he was murdered in the Yemen and, as all his notes were lost, he has never received in full the recognition that he deserved.

We have seen that in 1811 Muhammad Ali of Egypt invaded Arabia to crush the house of Saud. Many Europeans accompanied his armies in various capacities but few attained the eminence of the Scottish drummer-boy, Thomas Keith who as Ibrahim Agha was appointed Governor of Medina. Another soldier was Giovanni Finati

From the middle ages until this century the pilgrim caravans from Cairo and Damascus were led by the *Mahmal*—an emblem of royalty. This was a litter of rich brocade, decorated with gold and silver and containing nothing but two copies of the Quran in silver boxes. The *Mahmal* was present at the great ceremonies like the sermon on Jabal Arafat. The camel which carried it was excused from work for the remainder of its days. Here we see the *Mahmal* passing through the streets of Mecca.

of Ferrara who had been destined for the Church. He was called up for the Napoleonic forces and deserted three times, the last occasion being in the Balkans when he and some companions including their Sergeant's wife, took refuge with the Turks. Finati became a Muslim and was appointed pipe-bearer to a General, but, having seduced his master's wife, deemed it prudent to desert once again. He went to Egypt and enlisted in the army. He was on duty during the massacre of the Mameluks but his activities seem to have been confined to looting a handsome saddle and a still more handsome slave girl. He was posted to Arabia, but after being on the losing side in two savage battles, decided to desert in order, he claimed, to acquaint the Pasha with the incompetence of his generals. He was helped by friendly Beduins and reached Mecca which he thought 'neither large nor beautiful in itself [but] there is something in it that is calculated to impress a sort of awe'.

For nearly six days he stood outside a house occupied by Muhammad Ali, holding aloft a poster which set out his demand for an interview. He was eventually well received and after a couple more battles (this time on the winning side), he caught the plague and was evacuated to Egypt. He tok advantage of a mutiny to loot a huge chest which when opened proved merely to contain cheap crockery of insufficient value to pay the wages of the porters that he had all too optimistically engaged. His tale, however, ends happily, for he fell in with William Bankes, a wealthy English dilettante whom he accompanied as interpreter through Nubia, Palestine and Syria before reaching Britain where he was 'pleased with the simple manners of the Welsh villagers'. Finati's cheerful, picaresque account forms an agreeable contrast to those solemn scholars or enthusiasts who have also visited Mecca.

A much more reputable character was Maurice Tamisier, who served as a doctor in the armies of Muhammad Ali. At the end of 1833 he had a very rough voyage to Jedda during which he chivalrously intervened when a fellow passenger swore to divorce his wife who had just been seasick over his lunch and his beard. Accompanied by a group of other Europeans, including an amateur conjurer whose tricks astonished the Beduins, and an Italian opera singer whose talents were less appreciated, he made his way into the mountainous area of Asir in the south of the Hejaz, and took part in a battle in which Egyptian troops were rewarded with 10 shillings for every pair of enemy ears that they brought in. Tamisier obviously enjoyed chatting to the local people and recorded some of their tales. He heard for example that the Arabian cow has a hump because once the Prophet was so tired that he mounted one and instantly the animal grew a hump to make the experienced camel rider comfortable. He remarked on the intimate relationship between a Beduin and his camel for, when content, the Arab would serenade it with affectionate or even amorous songs to which it reacted with pleasure: if angry he might go so far as to denounce it as a Christian, at which abuse the brute would manifest a decent sense of shame.

Few of the travellers to Mecca had a stranger history than Léon Roches who, after a legal education, became one of the earliest settlers in newly-conquered Algeria. There in his early twenties he fell in love with a fourteen year old Arab girl whose family could never have contemplated her marriage to a Christian. He saw her but half a dozen times and only once alone but this passion dominated his life. He resolved to work for concord between the French invaders and the heroic Emir Abd al-Qadr who led the resistance. He posed, therefore, as a convert to Islam and took service with the Emir, one of whose closest advisers he became. He carried out various perilous missions during one of which he learned that his adored Khadijah had died, saying that she had returned his love. He now wished only for death and was in this mood when war broke out again. He felt that he could not bear arms against his fellow-countrymen so he boldly proclaimed to the Emir that he was no Muslim. The punishment for apostasy from Islam has always been death but Abd al-Qadr, seeing that no one else had overheard this blasphemy, merely said 'Go! I leave the punishment of your soul to God. Let your body disappear from my sight.'

Roches decided to risk his life in an attempt to bring about a reconciliation between the two peoples in Algeria and felt that this could best be done by getting a declaration from the highest Muslim legal authorities that it .was no sin for the Faithful to live under Christian domination and that they were not bound to sacrifice themselves by resisting overwhelming force. To obtain such a document he went firstly to Tunis, then to Cairo and finally to Mecca where he arrived in December 1841.

Despite his perfect Arabic, Roches decided to pose as a European convert to Islam and was fortunate to meet a highly respected Algerian Doctor of Law with whom he agreed to share the expenses of the journey. He spent three days in Medina where he was enchanted by the sight of the Prophet's Mosque by night with its myriad lamps bringing out the beauty of magnificent carpets and gilded inscriptions. After a fortnight in Mecca he went up to Taif to interview the Grand Sharif. The Sharif, by temperament a politician rather than a religious leader, was more interested in Roches' position as a diplomatic agent of France than in the question of whether he were a

The camp on Jabal Arafat before the Sermon, photographed in 1889 by the Dutch traveller, Hurgronje.

genuine Muslim. Concluding his business satisfactorily, Roches returned to take part in the rites of the pilgrimage, feeling tremendously drawn towards Islam but still convinced that he could never be anything but a Christian.

Roches was on his way to the culmination of the *haj* – the sermon at Arafat – when suddenly he encountered two Algerians whom, as a government official he had previously imprisoned. They saluted him politely but he felt as if he had trodden on a venomous snake and hoped desperately to lose himself amongst the mass of 60,000 pilgrims. Suddenly he heard the cry 'There is the Christian! Seize the infidel son of an infidel!' He felt that his last moment had come as a group of men converged upon him. They gagged and bound him and placed him on a camel: it was not for some time that he learned that his captors were in fact soldiers that the Sharif had sent to save the emissary of France from the hands of an outraged mob which would have certainly killed him. His escort seem to have beaten records in getting him to Jedda in less than six hours and there they commandeered a boat to remove him from the country.

The Manakha or camping ground of the pilgrims at Medina, with the great medieval fort beyond it in the middle and another fort on the hill in the distance.

Three months after completing the pilgrimage to Mecca Roches spent Easter in Rome, and, hurling himself upon the tomb of St Peter, resolved to become a priest. He was eventually persuaded to renounce his hope and returned to Algeria. He ended a distinguished career as Ambassador to Japan.

Nearly twenty years later another Christian in Mecca had an experience almost as frightening as that of Léon Roches. The Baron Heinrich von Maltzan was thirty-four and in 1860 he had been travelling in the Arab world for a decade. Among his friends was an Algerian with a gargantuan appetite for hashish, who, in return for a supply guaranteed to last six months, allowed von Maltzan to use his name on a passport to Mecca for the pilgrimage.

Apart from his first night in Jedda – he found a hotel which seemed incredibly cheap until he discovered that it was next to a monastery of howling Dervishes who shrieked all night – he reached Mecca without incident. He was totally unimpressed, and indeed disturbed: he regarded the rites as boring and even lunatic and he compared the Great Mosque to a citadel of Demons. He had just returned from Arafat when he overheard two genuine Algerians discussing him and concluding that he was a Christian in disguise. Von Maltzan left Mecca almost as rapidly as Roches had done. He returned the passport, duly stamped, to his hashish-addicted friend who, for the rest of his days, was certain that he had made the pilgrimage himself but could not for the life of him remember any detail of it.

On 25 August 1862 a letter headed 'The Mecca Pilgrimage' appeared in *The Times* over the signature of Hajji Muhammad Abd al-Wahid of Norwood. This title concealed the identity of Dr Herman Bicknell, once of St Bartholomew's Hospital and later an Army Surgeon in India. He had already travelled in Java, Tibet and the Himalayas and became convinced that it would be for the benefit of the British Empire if more Englishmen could gain the knowledge of Islam that the *haj* would bring. He therefore posed as a British convert and made the greater part of the journey in European dress, unsuitable though it was for the Red Sea. Although the Great Mosque only reminded him of the Palais Royal in Paris, he duly performed all the rites – but excused himself from going on to Medina because of the heat. His account ended by recommending an obliging guide in Mecca 'who has promised to show to other Englishmen the same politeness which I experienced from his hands'. He felt that previous visitors had made things unnecessarily difficult for themselves by going in disguise although 'it is absolutely indispensable to be a Mussulman (at least externally) and to have an Arabic name'. After his return he explored the Andes and the Arctic and died in his early forties after an accident on the Matterhorn.

Fifteen years after Bicknell another Englishman entered Mecca. John Fryer Keane was the son of a clergyman and had run away to sea at the age of twelve. He spent

Medina. A square in the old city.

most of the next nine years among Muslims, mainly as an officer on ships with Indian crews. He arrived at Jedda, attached himself to the suite of an Indian prince and after six weeks in Mecca felt as completely at home as if he had been there all his life. No one commented upon his fair skin for, as he said, the visitors were so varied that it looked like Madame Tussaud's out for a walk and the spectacle of the Archbishop of Canterbury in a mitre would really have caused no comment. He wandered around happily, peering in through a school window to see the boys having the soles of their feet beaten in batches of five and chattering with a Muslim lady who, as Miss McIntosh, had been taken prisoner during the Indian Mutiny.

He was deeply impressed by the religious sincerity of the pilgrims and the deep spirituality that it engendered, but he cared much less for the resident population. All, he said, were beggars: ' ''Bakshish'' roars the camel; ''backshish'' brays the ass; ''backshish'' yelps the cur, till, after passing through a stage where you fancy you hear nothing else, you get so accustomed to it, that it costs you an effort of will to hear it.' His dislike for them was increased when one day he was wandering around as 'an Eastern swell' in a bright white tunic and a huge turban, a child for no apparent reason said 'Look at that Christian.' A loafer, in the hope of gain, demanded a profession of faith from him and Keane seized his shoulders, spun him round and delivered a solid kick – 'I could not have perpetrated a more un-Muhammadan act.' A crowd started to stone him so, snatching up a child as a shield, he made for the local police station. There he claimed to be a Muslim and his fluency in cursing convinced the authorities who escorted him back to his lodgings.

Keane's troubles were not yet over. He went on to Medina and on the way was settling down to a tasty stew when a Beduin, who had just finished a particularly revolting operation on his camel, approached and after wiping his hands on 'his offensive mat of hair', plunged 'his loathsome paw slap into the middle' of the Englishman's dish. In a frenzy of rage, Keane hurled the plate at the Arab with such violence that it knocked him

Burton described the Ferrash as free citizens who did weekly tours of duty, attending to the maintenance of the Prophet's tomb. Other functions were performed by eunuchs who enjoyed great respect when they travelled beyond the city. This drawing of a Ferrash was published in 1790.

down. A few moments later the Beduin crept up upon him and thrust a spear so deeply into his leg that he almost bled to death on the spot. A last memory before losing consciousness was that of three vultures wheeling optimistically above. However, a local wise man plugged the wound with raw cotton and not long afterwards Keane was able to walk into Medina. Medina, he thought, ranked at first sight with Constantinople for beauty but on further acquaintance he, like Burton, found the Prophet's Mosque tawdry.

After his return he wrote in his autobiography, 'I had performed the fearfully risky pilgrimage to Mecca with but one purpose: and that was by performing a feat to bring my name forward as a capable traveller, it would stand me in good stead as recommendation for the support and means I should require to advance my long-cherished designs on Papua.' It is not clear if he ever achieved this ambition but during the next few years he was imprisoned in Brazil, edited a newspaper in Shanghai, worked for the Indian Railways, prospected in Burma and lived as a tramp in England. He was last heard of cutting sugarcane in Queensland. His books are lively and full of arresting turns of phrase: it is not difficult to visualize the beauty of the lady whose face looked like 'three kicks in a mud wall'.

None of the Christians who have dwelt in Mecca knew the city as well as the Dutchman, Christian Snouck Hurgronje, who spent more than six months there in 1885 after having already lived for five months in Jedda. He was a scholar of Semitic languages, obtained his Doctorate with a thesis on the origins of the *haj* and became a lecturer in Islamic institutions at the college in which the government trained future officials for service in the predominantly Muslim East Indies. He felt it important to study the influences to which the Javanese were subjected in Mecca and the details of the social institutions of their religion. Hurgronje was helped in his research by contracting a local marriage (he seems to have used the same method everywhere he worked) and his wife brought him much information that he could never otherwise have obtained. He was able to describe, and even to photograph the extraordinary costume of a Meccan bride with her headdress looking like an entire jeweller's shop full of brooches and her dress covered with silk pads studded with countless ornaments so that even the poorest could hardly move. He learned, also, how women treat their children's illnesses by putting under their pillow seven loaves which were later given to the dogs – a cure which hardly ever seemed to work.

James Silk Buckingham (1786–1855) was the first of the Romantic explorers of Arabia. His predecessors were strictly factual but he pioneered a new 'impressionistic' style and was interested in his own reactions. Later he was a Member of Parliament and President of the London Temperance Society.

Hurgronje made a detailed study of the local phenomenon of *Zar* – diabolic possession which he found 'just as much a necessity of life to most women as tobacco or the gold or gilded embroidery of their trousers'. Many used it as an excuse to plead that a new dress or jewellery was essential for their recovery and exorcism parties were noted for their jollity. One of Hurgronje's friends was a Doctor whose wife felt that she, like all her friends, had a right to a *Zar*: her husband pretended to consult a new textbook and to discover that branding with hot irons was the best cure. The lady rapidly recovered.

It is not known how long Snouck Hurgronje would have wished to stay in Mecca but through no fault of his own he became involved in international intrigue over the case of the Teima Stone (page 000). It became the object of the French to have him out of the way and their Consul leaked the fact of his presence in Mecca. He had to leave in a hurry but for another fifty years he remained one of the greatest experts in the world on Islam.

In 1894 a second French Algerian followed Roches to Mecca. This was a professional photographer Gervais-Courtellemont whose Muslim friends encouraged him to go because they felt that it would increase his understanding of their psychology. He had already written 'I love Islam in its simple faith and I admire, without daring to share it, its unshakable hope.' He had no particular difficulties even when he took photographs, explaining that what he was using was a sort of binoculars: 'I know,' said his guide, 'that you call it a camera because I have often seen tourists using it in Tangier.' His book contains the story of the phantom camels which arrive nightly in Mecca: it is certain that all buried in the Holy City will rise to glory on the last day but those unworthy are

Drawn & Etched by W.L. Brooke A.R.M.A.   Aquatinted by R. Havell Jun.

Portrait of the Author J. S. Buckingham

in the Costume worn in his Travels.

Published by Henry Colburn London Oct. 1829.

removed by these beasts and replaced by those more deserving from as far away as Morocco or Turkestan. He wrote also of the difficulty of buying jewellery, for each purchase had to be approved by the shaikh of the Goldsmiths' Guild who measured the article against a complicated array of date stones and beans and decreed an official price. He described also a special sort of silver ring which can only be bought in Mecca: for a non-*Hajji* to wear one would be the equivalent of appearing in school colours to which one was not entitled.

Three more Englishmen visited Mecca before the First World War – two genuine Muslims who spent most of their lives in the Faith and an adventurous Army Officer in disguise. Chronologically the first was Hajji Abdallah Williamson who made his first pilgrimage about 1895. Like Keane he had run away to sea and then had a series of adventures as a gold-miner in California, a whale-hunter in the Arctic and a rebel in the Philippines. While serving as a policeman in Aden in the 1890s he became a Muslim and was encouraged to settle elsewhere. For the next twenty years he lived near Basra, surprising the local people by riding a penny-farthing and scaring them almost out of their wits with a gramophone: they were certain that it was a box of devils. Many times he went raiding with the Beduins and he won a great reputation as a fine judge of camel-flesh. As a change he bought a dhow and certainly engaged in pearling, probably in gun-running and possibly in the slave trade. After a period working for the British after the conquest of Iraq he ended his varied career respectably enough as an interpreter and explorer for what is now British Petroleum.

Hedley Churchward, whose tale is told under the splendid title of *From Drury Lane to Mecca*, worked as a theatrical designer in the 1880s, producing back-cloths for Lillie Langtry and Henry Irving. His skill won him invitations to Sandringham to make sets for royal theatricals and he acted as impresario at the opening of the Manchester Ship Canal. A visit to Morocco turned him into a Muslim and he settled in Cairo with an Egyptian wife. He studied theology at al-Azhar, the 1000-year-old university which is the greatest intellectual centre of

The oryx is a lovely antelope nearly as large as a cow. With the use of modern rifles by hunters—and later of jeeps and machine guns it became almost extinct. However there is now a fine herd being reared in captivity by H. E. Shaikh Jasim bin Hamad al-Thani, Minister of Education of Qatar.

Islam, and was declared a genuine convert by the highest spiritual authorities. He made the *haj* in 1910 and calculated the entire cost, including five months in Mecca, at £400.

The Army Officer, in Mecca two years before Churchward, was Arthur Wavell, cousin and school-fellow of the future Field Marshal. He had served as a young subaltern in the Boer War and remained working there for the military survey, passing eighteen months without seeing a European. In 1906 he started a sisal plantation in Kenya and having learned Swahili came much in contact with the local Muslims, one of whom he took to Mecca. His object, he wrote, was partly to gratify his curiosity and partly to qualify himself to explore more inaccessible parts of the Peninsula by learning about Arab ways and by gaining the title of *Hajji*. For £3.10s. he bought a third-class ticket from Damascus to Medina on the new railway. His three weeks there were uneventful except for occasional sniping by disgruntled Beduin at the Turkish garrison. In Mecca he hired a house for £7 a month and came to the conclusion that provided one entered the country in disguise, knew something about Islam and behaved discreetly, the enterprise was without 'any risk worth mentioning'.

Indeed Wavell was in greater danger two years later when he went to the Yemen. Owing to chronic insecurity, the Turkish authorities at Hodeidah refused to allow him to go up to Sanaa but he managed to slip secretly out of the port. The attitude of the Turks was proved not unreasonable, for a few days after his arrival a large force of Arabs equipped with erratic and therefore extremely dangerous field guns started to besiege the capital. The military leaders, sure that Wavell was a spy, kept him under constant surveillance and as soon as the city was relieved, after four months, determined to send him back to the coast under guard. Wavell, however, was resolved to see more of the Yemen and arranged for a well-recommended and experienced bandit to escort him to Marib. Wearing a shirt of mail under his clothes, he escaped from Sanaa but found that his confederate was not at the rendezvous. Wavell was recaptured and followed to the Governor's

John Fryer Keane lost
consciousness with three of
these griffon vultures hopefully
hovering. The horror of their
approach to a helpless victim is
said to be increased by the
foulness of their breath. The
clean white bones of camels and
donkeys along any track in
Arabia testifies to their
efficiency. From a watercolour
by Charles Whymper. R. G.
Searight Esq, London.

palace by a gleeful crowd that anticipated that it would
shortly be entertained by the sight of a public execution
but after a short period in jail he was expelled from the
country. In the autumn of 1914 he was back in Kenya and
raised a force of Arab water carriers which played a vital
part in repelling a German attack on Mombasa. In January
1916 he was killed in action in East Africa.

Knowledge of the northern Hejaz increased rapidly
after the beginning of the present century. Engineers
mapped parts of it for the Hejaz Railway and scholars
found their way to the great ruins of Madain Salih. In
1909 Douglas Carruthers, a naturalist who had already
been in the Congo and in Turkestan and was later to go to
Mongolia, wandered around in search of the Arabian
oryx. This magnificent white antelope, almost as large as a
cow, had long been in danger of extinction – a fate which
had already befallen the ostrich and the wild ass which
used to frequent the same areas. In weeks of hunting he
found only two and managed to bring back their skins.
However he enjoyed himself with his Beduin guides and
thought that they liked him – 'the wilder that Arab of the

Of the numerous portraits of T. E. Lawrence (1888–1935), this one by Augustus John comes nearest to hinting at his elusive character. National Portrait Gallery, London.

Desert the quicker he is to recognize and love a sahib!'

There was danger when 'a whole cavalcade of half-naked horsemen, riding bare-backed, armed with lances and rifles, came like a whirlwind' and took him prisoner. After a period of tension when he thought that they might even loot his trousers, and more precious still his oryx skins, his companions secured the release of the party. Like other travellers he thought that the Nafud was the most impressive natural phenomenon that he had ever seen – 'The colour of the sands, from a distance is pure carmine in a low morning light, changing under the midday glare to white, and at dusk they appear wine red and of an intangible velvety texture. But at close quarters the sands are every shade of yellow and red, blending softly into an amazing mixture for which one can find no name.'

The war brought many Europeans to the Hejaz of whom Lawrence is of course the best-known. He is not a man that one can discuss in a few words in a book such as this but the present writer believes that long before 1914 he was a highly professional Intelligence officer. His unpublished writings are models of military reporting. Here it is proposed to quote three passages from *The Seven Pillars of Wisdom* in an attempt to persuade people to read the work as a whole.

'The men received me cheerfully. Beneath every great rock or bush they sprawled like lazy scorpions, resting from the heat, and refreshing their brown limbs with the early coolness of the shaded stone. Because of my khaki they took me for a Turkish-trained officer who had deserted to them, and were profuse in good-humoured but ghastly suggestions of how they should treat me. Most of them were young, though the term "fighting man" in the Hejaz meant anyone between twelve and sixty sane enough to shoot. They were a tough-looking crowd, dark-coloured, some negroid. They were physically thin, but exquisitely made, moving with an oiled activity altogether delightful to watch. It did not seem possible that men could be hardier or harder. They would ride immense distances day after day, run through sand and over rocks bare-foot in the heat for hours without pain, and climb their hills like goats. Their clothing was

135

Jules Gervais-Courtellemont
(1863–1931) was a pioneer of
photographic journalism. Apart
from his visit to Mecca in 1894,
he travelled widely in China and
was a passenger on the first train
into Medina. He photographed
the inauguration of the Hejaz
railway in 1908 (*opposite*).

mainly a loose shirt, with sometimes short cotton drawers, a head shawl usually of red cloth, which acted as
towel or handkerchief or sack as required. They were
corrugated with bandoliers, and fired joy-shots when
they could.'

'Jizil was a deep gorge some two hundred yards in
width . . . The walls each side were of regular bands of
sandstone, streaked red in many shades. The union of
dark cliffs, pink floors, and pale green shrubbery was
beautiful to eyes sated with months of sunlight and sooty
shadow. When evening came, the declining sun crim-
soned one side of the valley with its glow, leaving the
other in purple gloom.'

Writing of the Plain of El Houl, east of Tabuk, he says:
'We rode in it without seeing signs of life; no tracks of
gazelle, no lizards, no burrowing of rats, not even of
birds. We, ourselves, felt tiny in it, and our urgent
progress across its immensity was a stillness or immobility
of futile effort. The only sounds were the hollow echoes,
like the shutting down of pavements over vaulted places,
of rotten stone slab when they tilted under our camels'
feet, and the low but piercing rustle of the sand, as it crept
slowly westward before the hot wind along the worn
sandstone . . . By noon it blew a half-gale, so dry that our
shrivelled lips cracked open, and the skin of our faces
chapped; while our eye-lids, gone granular, seemed to
creep back and bare our shrinking eyes.'

We may conclude this chapter with a mention of two
English ladies who went to the Hejaz after the First World
War. One whose story appeared under the name of
Countess Malmignati took large Christmas crackers as
presents for the simple natives. Her book, with chapters
such as 'Amongst fanatical Arabs' reads like the script of a
minor film. The second, Lady Evelyn Cobbold, claimed to
have been the first European woman to have performed
the *haj*. She seems to have had a splendid time and was
able to find many upper class ladies with whom she could
take tea and engage in polite conversation. Her cosy
Mecca is very different from the one in which so many of
the earlier travellers that we have mentioned had had to
fear for their lives.

137

Travellers in Eastern and Northern Arabia

EVEN ARAB geographers had comparatively little to say about the northern and eastern areas of the Peninsula, and Niebuhr and Burckhardt were able to obtain a little information only by hearsay. Most of the important centres of western and southern Arabia had been visited by Europeans by 1800, but none had penetrated more than a few miles inland from the east coast. The first to do so was Captain George Forster Sadlier of the 47th Foot.

We have seen that in February 1818 Ibrahim Pasha had captured the Saudi capital of Diriyyah at a time when pirates were plaguing British commerce in the Gulf. By January 1819 the authorities in India conceived the idea of writing to congratulate the Pasha and to invite his co-operation to wipe out the marauders: by mid-April Sadlier was instructed that His Excellency, 'having the most perfect reliance in your prudence and discretion, has been pleased to confide the execution of this important task to you'.

In June, after a halt at Muscat trying to persuade the Sayyid to join the proposed alliance, Sadlier arrived at Qatif. No one knew exactly where Ibrahim was, but it seemed possible that he might be at Hufuf, a few days' journey inland. Sadlier procured an Arab escort and set out to find him. He had trouble with his companions almost from the beginning and wrote with exasperation in his diary 'the procrastination, duplicity, falsity, deception, and fraudulence of the Beduin cannot be described by one to a European in language which would present to his mind the real character of these hordes of robbers. To attempt to argue with them on the principles of justice, right or equity is ridiculous; and to attempt to insist upon their adhering to promises or agreements is equally fruitless, unless you possess the means of enforcing compliance'. He discovered that the art of his guide was to appear meek until the party was well into the desert and then 'his conduct was that of a barbarian who had got his prey in his power, and determined not to lose the opportunity lest another so favourable should not offer. We had no water, nor could we procure any. I was happy to put an end to the uproar by paying 60 dollars.'

All that he found at Hufuf was 'a few bad apricots, figs very hard and dry, bad water-melons; the onions had the shape of carrots'. What no one knew was that the Pasha was withdrawing from Nejd: his local commander was certain that Ibrahim was encamped a few days' march to the west and, as he was sending a convoy, Sadlier decided to accompany it. When the party reached its objective, it was greeted with the news that Ibrahim had recently moved to a new base at Rass, right in the centre of Arabia.

As Rass was not too far away, Sadlier decided to go on there – and arrived to hear that his quarry had left two days before for Medina. Sadlier felt that he had done all that could be reasonably be required of him and that he should turn back to Basra where he knew that he would find a British ship. The local commander said that this would be totally impossible without a large escort which he lacked the authority to provide. Willy-nilly Sadlier continued his westward route. At Medina, eleven weeks after leaving Qatif, he was cordially received by Ibrahim. The Pasha expressed delight with the sword of honour that Sadlier had brought but regretted that as a simple soldier he could not discuss the political aspects of his mission. Sadlier could not enter Medina but skirted the city on the way to Yanbu, where he became the first European to have crossed the Peninsula from coast to coast.

He sailed down to Jedda where he had arranged a second meeting with the Pasha and where his mission ended in a flaming row. Ibrahim had decided to send two horses to the Governor General but Sadlier noticed that the saddles were distinctly second-hand and sent them back. Ibrahim cancelled the presents and ordered him to leave at once. Sadlier refused to go except on a British ship and had to spend another three months in Jedda before one arrived.

Sadlier's crossing of Arabia was not to be repeated for another century but of all the travellers in this book, he had fewest of the qualities of an explorer. He hated the country and he loathed the people: he was totally inflexible and refused the slightest concession to local customs or conditions. But however reluctant he may have been, he was a conscientious officer and brought back much geographical information of great value.

Our next character could hardly have been more different from the unwilling and unsympathetic Sadlier. Georg August Wallin, a Finn born in 1811, decided from his youth that his vocation was to be Arabian travel. He wrote a doctoral dissertation in Latin on 'The Chief Differences between Classical and Modern Arabic' and then obtained a grant for a comparative study of dialects. He decided to pass as a doctor and vaccinator and spent a further six months mastering these trades. In January 1844 he arrived in Cairo where he remained for a year studying calligraphy and theology, playing the Arab flute, and intoning the Quran. He had no difficulty in passing as a Muslim, was a meticulous observer and developed an excellent technique for taking notes without being seen. He was interested in everything: tribal politics, ancient inscriptions, topography, botany, etc.

Qatif. When he landed here in 1819, Sadlier little knew that he would be the first European to cross the Arabian Peninsula.

140

Unfortunately the only accounts available in English are two articles which are bare lists of facts and do not lend themselves to quotation.

In April 1845 he left for Palestine as he felt that entering Arabia from the north would be least likely to attract attention. He became, in September, the first European to enter Hail where the ruling family, the Ibn Rashids, practiced the most princely hospitality and all comers were lodged and fed for as long as they wished without charge or question. It must have been expensive for them for the people said that the water was so good that one could eat an entire sheep without indigestion, provided that it was washed down with a drink from the local wells. He spent two happy months there but found that it was impossible to carry out his original intention of going on to Riyadh because the route was insecure and he lacked money. Although he had thought that it would be 'childish vanity' to go on to Mecca, which had already been adequately described, he decided to attach himself to a caravan of Persian pilgrims and go on down to the coast from Medina. When the time came, he felt too ill and was too poor to leave his comrades so he went on to make the *haj*. A few days after that he entered Jedda with a shilling in his pocket.

Wallin returned to Cairo and resumed his studies. Three years later he landed on the Red Sea coast just south of Sinai, and after wandering for two months where no European had ever been, came again to Hail. He had been careful never to harm generous hosts by eating much of their limited food and gave in return little presents of coffee and tobacco. He was again disappointed of reaching Riyadh for a friendly member of the Ibn Rashids warned him that he was suspected of being a Christian. Hurriedly he joined a party going to Baghdad. By the time he reached Basra he was penniless. 'I had to avoid acquaintances, deny myself fruit and candles, wear dirty clothes or wash them without soap . . . I found my only pleasure in the laments of discontented Persian poets.' Finally he was rescued by the Royal Navy and helped to return to Cairo. He gave up his project of seeing the Yemen and in 1850 returned to Helsingfors (Helsinki)

University as Professor of Oriental Languages. Two years later, while planning another visit to Arabia, he died. All agree that he ranks as one of the greatest of all Arabian explorers.

We have seen that in 1862 Napoleon III sent the Englishman Palgrave into Nejd: two years later he sent an Italian into the same area. This was Carlo Guarmani, who was born in Leghorn in 1828 but had lived in the Levant since 1850 as the agent of the French Postal Service in Jerusalem. Whenever possible he wandered with the nomadic tribes of Transjordan and became a specialist on horses. He obtained a commission to buy stallions for the royal studs of Paris and Turin and set out, accompanied by an old retainer 'releasing myself from the embraces of my sorrowful family . . . who thought I was on the way to a voluntary execution.' He passed as Khalil Aga, Master of the Horse to the Pasha of Damascus.

He was already on good terms with many of the tribal leaders in the area and encountered little difficulty. He showed his understanding of Beduin ways when the encampment blew down: his townsman servant was about to help the women to re-erect the tents but Guarmani stopped him – no tribesman would have demeaned himself by putting a hand to this female task. He was successful in buying three prime stallions for the large price of 100 camels but he was never allowed near the more precious mares for he might have had the evil eye. Several times the party was attacked but 'my post was in the safest hiding-place, with the wounded, the women and the baggage'.

Inner Arabia was in a ferment of tribal warfare and near Unayzah he stumbled across a raiding party led by the Emir Abdallah whom we have already met in company with Palgrave. Abdallah refused to receive his unwilling visitor and sent him under escort to Hail where his first sight was of the rotting corpse of a Persian Jew who had been slaughtered for refusing to praise the Prophet. Guarmani resolved 'not to be amongst the poor in spirit and enter Paradise with the fools', but even if Talal ibn Rashid saw through his disguise as a Muslim Turk, he treated him with courtesy. Like Palgrave, Guarmani

paints a most favourable picture of the ruler of Jabal
Shammar whom he saw dispensing justice 'seated on the
western side of the mosque with his chief officials sitting
on his left, according to their rank, in rows one behind
another. Twenty slaves and servants sat in a semi-circle
on the ground in front of him, all well dressed in fine
black abahs, with red or blue cloth coats heavily
embroidered with gold; in their hands they held, as did
the prince and all his followers, a scimitar in a silver
scabbard'. The first case concerned an old woman who
complained that a local governor had taken her ass: two
soldiers were sent to seize his best animal and give it to the
plaintiff and to ensure that he also gave her a new suit of
clothes.

Guarmani obviously enjoyed himself, although as a
Victorian he was compelled to denounce 'customs and
habits of the worst type, the men being dissolute and the
women caring only for pleasure and luxury'. This did not,
however, prevent him from noticing that these women's
figures 'for purity of line . . . rivalled the most graceful
creations of Canova' with 'their long glossy black hair
oiled with an odourless pomade composed of finely
powdered palm bark and clarified fat obtained from
sheeps' tails'. He also thought that the neighbourhood,
under Talal's firm rule, safer than Italy, and he travelled
widely looking for horses. This security was only local,
for on the very last lap of the journey, Guarmani was

uwait has always been peaceful
nd devoted to commerce.
ravellers never seem to have
ad any misadventures there,
either in the booming modern
ty nor in the old Kuwait seen
ere.

attacked by a large *ghazzu* (tribal raiding party) and was lucky to save his horses and his life.

Nearly fifty years after Sadlier, another British officer came into Nejd. Almost since the beginning of his second reign, British relations with the Imam Faysal ibn Saud had been difficult: there had been actual armed clashes and the Saudis particularly resented the efforts of the Royal Navy to stamp out the slave trade which, of course, was not illegal under Muslim law. Colonel Lewis Pelly, the Resident in the Gulf, decided to try to establish friendly personal contact with the most feared and respected potentate in the area. He was also stimulated by the view of the Royal Geographical Society that no European could go safely to Riyadh (indeed its exact position was uncertain): no more was known of parts of the country than in the time of Ptolemy. Pelly was moreover keen to add to the laurels that he had won by a solo ride from Teheran to India by way of Kandahar.

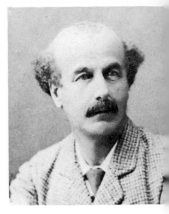

Sir Lewis Pelly (1825–92). His period from 1862 to 1873 as Political Resident in the Gulf marked a change in British policy. Before his time the authorities were mainly concerned with keeping the maritime peace: after it there were some efforts to better the lot of the inhabitants.

He went to Kuwait early in 1865 and applied for permission to advance. He spent the interval chatting and hunting with a local notable of whom he said 'no English gentleman could have been more unobtrusively courteous and hospitable'. Kuwait appears little in travel accounts of the time for there was nothing wild or romantic about it; a community of intelligent civilized merchants led by an enlightened ruling family and a place where the visitor experienced neither adventure nor disaster.

After some weeks a laconic note from the Imam told Pelly that he might enter Nejd but no guide accompanied the message. The party consisted of thirty camels carrying a Naval officer to undertake astronomical observations, a surgeon, an interpreter, three Indian orderlies, a Persian servant and a Portuguese cook and provisions of preserved soups and meat, dates and rice. Pelly insisted that they should wear Arab cloaks and thought that 'we looked much the sort of company that Falstaff would have objected to marching through Coventry with'.

The route was through complete desert (over what is now one of the richest oilfields in the world) and almost the most noteworthy event of the first ten days was the

Hawking is the great sport of eastern Arabia, with hares or gazelles for game. Today a good-looking peregrine may be worth £1000 untrained. A hawk is normally released at the end of the hunting season.

sight of a tree. Pelly seems to have spent most of his time questioning his escort and he amassed a great deal of information: he provided the first account of the Sulayb, the gypsies of the desert who are regarded as outcasts. No Beduin would deign to plunder them, no ruler to receive their tribute, no Arab to marry their women. They practiced religious rites connected with the North Star and did such smithying and tinkering as was needed among the nomads. They were particularly noted for their skill at hunting – it was said that by covering their heads with a gazelle skin, they could approach within a few yards of a grazing herd.

After a fortnight they saw the first building and the first cultivation since leaving Kuwait, and two days later they entered Riyadh. Their reception was polite but cool, and Faysal proved to be a man of apparently seventy years, of immense presence, and quite blind. 'His voice was well modulated, and his words calm and measured. He was dignified, almost gentle; yet you felt he could be remorselessly cruel.' He started by remarking that Riyadh was a strange place for a European to visit and none had ever done so before. He spoke not unfavourably of the British Government but added 'We abominate your religion.' He prayed that the West in general and Pelly in particular might see the error of their ways.

On their next visit the Imam emerged from the harem,

145

One of the many tombs of Muslim saints which can be found in south-west Arabia. They are the centres of lively festivals. The descendants of the original saints have an important role in settling tribal disputes, and oaths are taken by people placing their hands on the walls of the tomb.

supported by two female slaves who, on the threshold, handed him over to two men. Intriguingly, Pelly says 'from something which occurred, I could not but presume that he was a freemason'. He expressed pleasure with the gifts that Pelly had brought – a rifle, a gold watch, some red cloth, a gilt pistol and a sword. The conversations were extremely cordial but some of the Imam's entourage became anxious to prevent a close relationship with an infidel power. The situation deteriorated rapidly and Pelly thought it prudent not to delay his departure. He reached the coast without incident and concluded an extremely successful career with a Knighthood, Membership of Parliament and an invitation from the King of the Belgians to become Administrator of the Congo.

All the visitors that we have mentioned so far crept into Hail in disguise: the next pair went without concealment as aristocrats making a social call upon another of their kind. Wilfrid Scawen Blunt was large and commanding and spoke fluent but ungrammatical Arabic while his wife, Lady Anne (a grand-daughter of Byron), was shy and mouselike and her Arabic so perfect and so classical that hardly anyone could understand a word that she said. Both had a passionate love of horses and an enthusiasm for Arabic literature, of which Wilfrid, a poet of distinction, produced translations which can still be read with pleasure. Wilfrid felt that the Arabs were his 'first love and in Algeria had contrasted the life of noble pastoral camelmen with that of wine-swilling, hog-guzzling Frenchmen'; throughout his life he was always anxious 'to bathe one's sick Western soul in the pure healing beauty of the East'.

On a previous visit to Syria, the Blunts had met a certain Muhammad ibn Aruk, who claimed to be descended from one of three brothers of an ancient family of Nejd who had fled the country together on a single camel. Each brother had stopped off in a different place and Muhammad was anxious to retrace the path of this famous ride in the hope of finding a cousin that he might claim as a bride. He was therefore quite happy to go to Hail.

They left Syria in December 1878 and had not gone very far when the Blunts, having wandered away from their companions, were captured by a tribal raiding party. Lady Anne was knocked down by a lance and Wilfrid had the stock of his gun broken over his head. The *ghazzu*, however, turned out to be friends of Muhammad ibn Aruk and the adventure ended with the two parties lunching amicably together. Indeed, as Lady Anne remarked, 'in spite of their rough behaviour we could see that they were gentlemen'.

At Jawf, Muhammad found a suitable cousin and after the Blunts had conducted all the negotiations and advanced the £50 necessary for the bride-price, became engaged to her. He continued with them and the next day 'we saw a red streak on the horizon before us which rose and gathered as we approached it, stretching out east and west in an unbroken line. It might have been taken for an effect of mirage, but on coming nearer we found it broken into billows, and but for its red colour not unlike a stormy sea seen from the shore, for it rose up, as the sea seems to rise, when the waves are high, above the level of the land.' This was the Nafud and 'what surprised us was its colour, that of rhubarb and magnesia, nothing at all like the sand that we had expected'.

Nine months after Doughty, the Blunts entered Hail and their reception was very different. The Emir, Muhammad ibn Rashid, who had personally knifed his nephew and cut off the feet of his cousins, leaving them to bleed to death, could hardly have been more courteous. 'His countenance recalled to us the portraits of Richard III, lean, sallow cheeks, much sunken, thin lips, with an expression of pain except when smiling, a thin black beard, well defined black knitted eyebrows, and remarkable eyes – eyes deep sunk and piercing, like the eyes of a hawk, but ever turning restlessly from one of our faces to the other, and then to those beside him. It was the very type of a conscience stricken face, or one which fears an assassin. His hands, too, were long and claw-like and never quiet for an instant.' He was gorgeously dressed and carried several gold-hilted daggers and a gold-hilted sword adorned with turquoises and rubies.

His ladies, who received Lady Anne, were no less magnificent. One had around her neck a mass of gold chains studded with turquoises and pearls and on her head a golden plate from which streamed pearls. Each had in her left nostril a gold ring about two inches in diameter which had to be removed when eating.

Everything about his court was princely, except for the rather vulgar way in which he delighted in displaying his wealth. He took them to his kitchen to see 7 monstrous cauldrons each capable of boiling three whole camels and told them that his daily meat bill was for 40 sheep or 7 camels to feed some 200 guests. He showed them his stables containing about 100 superb horses, casually explaining that those were the ones ridden by his slaves. He even had 'one of those toys called telephones, which were the fashion last year in Europe'. The Blunts had never seen one and two slaves obligingly demonstrated its use by standing a few yards apart and bellowing at each other through it.

They stayed about a fortnight and left with some Persian pilgrims returning home. Looking back, Lady Anne thought it 'without exception the most beautiful view I ever saw in my life'. We cannot follow here the later story of the Blunts, of their foundation of the famous Crabbet stud of Arab horses, of Wilfrid's emerging as such a violent opponent of all British policy that he went to jail, of his Byronic championship of the Egyptians, of his influence on younger poets: the journey to Hail was only a few months in a very full life.

Charles Huber, an Alsatian, who had just preceded the Blunts into Hail, was also well received by Muhammad ibn Rashid. On his way he had recorded numerous

On the island of Socotra, where
perpetual streams and green
meadows make a sharp contrast
to the rest of Arabia.

inscriptions, including that of the Teima Stone which had an important inscription in a language never before found in Arabia. In 1883 he returned, accompanied by a German archaeologist Julius Euting, and in Hail a surprising scene took place: Euting, challenged to show his strength hung upside down by one leg on a tree-trunk held by slaves. Despite these party tricks, the two travellers seem to have disliked each other intensely but they did succeed in buying the Teima Stone which is now one of the glories of the Louvre. They separated as soon as they could and Euting was attacked by Beduins and managed to escape by killing two of them. Huber was not so fortunate: he left his papers and the Stone at Hail and went off to Mecca. On his way back he was murdered by his guides and Ibn Rashid scrupulously sent all his possessions back to France. The people of Jabal Shammar must have formed an odd impression of Germans for their next visitor thought that Europeans were disgraced by assuming Arab dress and appeared in full Prussian uniform with sword and helmet.

Early in 1914, Hail received its second visit from an English lady. Gertrude Bell was forty-four and had

The Blunts also visited Hail, the capital of Jabal Shammar, about nine months after Doughty. The horses of the Emir, Ibn Rashid, were among the most famous in Arabia.

right
The Teima stone dates from the fifth century B.C. and is probably the most important Aramaic (the actual language of Christ) inscription found in Arabia. It records how a new deity, Salm, was introduced into Teima by his priest, who provided an endowment for a temple and established a hereditary priesthood. This picture of the side of the stone shows the God above and the priest at the altar below. Louvre, Paris.

far right
This Arab, photographed by Gerald de Gaury, resembles, as he remarks, 'a woodcut to illustrate Chaucer'.

already seen much of western Asia as well as being an early Alpinist. She bought twenty camels in Damascus, hired three cameleers and two other servants and left secretly, for she knew that neither British nor Turkish authorities would look kindly upon her enterprise. Once she was stopped by an Ottoman governor and after much argument, persuaded him to accept a paper saying that the administration should not be held responsible for anything that might befall her. Something nearly did for a few days later she was held up by a Beduin shaikh who, after receiving presents from her, privily suggested to her party that they should murder her and share the loot. She had a tiring journey, sometimes only doing a mile an hour through Nafud. She was not allowed to enter Hail but was accommodated in a guest-house outside the walls: She was worried about money, for although she had a draft for £200 this was made out to the State Treasurer who was absent with his master stealing camels. Finally some of her friends persuaded the Emir's formidable grandmother, who seemed to be the effective Chancellor of the Exchequer, to let her have some cash. She managed to pay a few visits and thought that the atmosphere of the

Although the once 'Pirate Coast' is now the Union of Arab Emirates, many of its inhabitants still lead practically amphibious lives – small boats serve as taxis in Dubai. Unfortunately the lovely square wind-towers are a more expensive means of cooling than air-conditioning and are being replaced.

harems could not have changed since the Middle Ages. Only on the last morning of her twelve-day stay was she permitted to stroll in the town. She made her way to Mesopotamia where she was to spend much of the rest of her life, firstly as tribal expert to the British occupation and then as Director of Antiquities.

Two men from central Europe attached themselves to the great Rualla tribe of northern Arabia and wandered with them before the war, perhaps as much as intelligence agents as scholars. Both Alois Musil and Carl Raswan claim to have been blood brothers of the redoubtable chief, Nuri Shaalan, who was believed to have killed seventy people with his own hand, including most of his brothers; but excluding Turks as hardly human. He was always prepared to repeat the performance and carried a revolver with 48 rounds and never put down his carbine for which he has 120 bullets strung around his body. Both described the unique standard of the tribe – a camel-borne litter adorned with ostrich feathers which served as a symbol of sovereignty and led the tribe into battle.

From each writer we may find scraps of information which illustrate the life of a nomadic tribe. Musil observed that anyone bitten by a mad dog was driven into the desert with supplies for forty days. If he was seen before the period ended, he was shot on sight. He told also how an Arab tribe prepares to cross a long waterless stretch of dunes: selected camels are coaxed into drinking up to seventy quarts of water, and then either their tongues are cut out, or their mouths are sewn up, for grazing would mix food with the water in their paunches. When required they can be slaughtered and the water extracted from their stomachs and it will be quite drinkable if left standing for a few hours. Raswan found that the only warm wash on a freezing morning was camel's urine. He returned after the war and claimed to have taken part in motorized *ghazzus*.

We have seen that during the period from 1900 to 1914, the mastery of Nejd passed from the Ibn Rashids of Hail back to the Ibn Sauds of Riyadh. It was now the latter city that travellers started to visit. One of the first to arrive was a Dane, Barclay Raunkaier, whose objective was to

examine the possibility of a second Royal Expedition that
would rival that of Niebuhr. In February 1912, at the age
of twenty-three, he left Kuwait with a caravan of 50 men
and 100 camels. This was the period in which the tribes
had become fanaticized and nowhere along the route was
the Christian made welcome. He found, as did Doughty,
that the most unfriendly reception was at Buraydah and
like him was nearly killed there by an intolerant population. The Governor did little to help him; 'the Emir is a
middle-aged man of singularly unprepossessing appearance. He has curly black hair, hanging unplaited. One eye
is sightless and filled with matter, the other seems to be
scowling, his lips are thick, the face is bloated and the

157

The game of *jarid* which Gerald de Gaury saw being practised a century after this drawing was made in 1838.

fingers swollen.' Despite the fact that Raunkaier had letters to his master, Ibn Saud, the Emir commandeered the visitor's revolver and binoculars.

Ibn Saud was away but his father Abd al-Rahman 'a marvellously handsome old man, whose whole appearance bears the mark of adventure and splendour' received his caller with elegance and no sign of surprise. He chatted about world politics with knowledge and then arranged for a caravan leader 'who breathes fanaticism and low intelligence' to take his guest back to the coast. Raunkaier had been ill throughout the journey and by now could scarcely stand, perhaps from the tuberculosis that was to kill him three years later. The ride was a nightmare: his guide stole the supplies that the Imam had provided and for four days Raunkaier never ate and drank only water so foul that he had to hold his nose. The party was passing through a dangerous area but his companions took no account of the fact and lit fires 'round which they dance with many strange contortions; at the same time they howl rather than sing an alternating double chant at the full pitch of their lung power'. He reached Hufuf in safety and Turkish officers gave him European comforts.

A few months after Raunkaier, an officer of the Royal Sussex Regiment, Gerald Leachman, entered Riyadh, on his second journey in Arabia. He had served in the Boer

Gertrude Bell (1868–1926) started travelling in the Middle East soon after leaving Oxford where she was the first girl to take First Class Honours in History. In 1916, a leading official stated 'it is generally admitted that she is the most knowledgeable person, male or female, in regard to all Arab questions'. She played a leading part in establishing Sharif Faysal as the first king of Iraq. National Portrait Gallery, London.

War and explored in Tibet before he wandered with the Anayzah tribe in 1909. He was in their camp of some 3500 tents when it was overwhelmed by an attack led by Ibn Rashid. The warriors fled, the women thrusting their jewellery into his hands for safe keeping while he remained sewing up the shoulder of a man who had been slashed open with a sword. Leachman was taken prisoner by the victors but treated as an honoured guest, enjoying the regal hospitality dispensed by the hereditary standard-bearer – an impressive figure in a coat of gold and with ten bullet wounds in his body. He stayed some months before being packed off to Basra. He decided to return to India by a circuitous route which took him on horseback through Kurdistan and Anatolia and ended with a dash, which became legendary, covering the 500 miles from Damascus to Baghdad on a camel in nine days. On his second visit he did not travel quite so fast but still averaged thirty miles a day from Damascus to Riyadh and the coast. The full political implications of his contact with Ibn Saud is still not clear. During the war, almost single-handed, by a mixture of ruthlessness, bluff and the art of appearing suddenly in impenetrable disguise, he prevented the desert tribes from attacking the western flank of the British advance in Mesopotamia. His murder in August 1920 was one of the first events of the Iraqi rising.

Ibn Saud's meeting with his next British visitor was certainly political. Captain Shakespear was the British Agent in Kuwait and he visited Riyadh in the course of what was to be the second crossing of Arabia from coast to coast. Near the end he was held up by the famous fighter Audah Abu Tayi – who was later to ride into Aqaba with Lawrence – and left with only £7. Lawrence said of Audah, 'when he dies, the Middle Ages of the desert will have ended'. As there is an account of his tearing out the heart of a vanquished foe to drink his blood, we may perhaps agree that he does not appear an ordinary man of the twentieth century.

After the war the motor car and then the aeroplane facilitated travel in Nejd and the work of Philby left little for other explorers to do. Arabian journeys were still far

159

from dull, however, as we may read in the delightful accounts of Gerald de Gaury. In the winter of 1935 he attended a fantasia in which Ibn Saud's sons, Saud and Faysal, who were to follow him on the throne, led tribesmen in a display of horsemanship: 'the parties rode away and took station opposite to each other, two or three groups on either side. They began to canter slowly round each other, while in front individual riders came out to play the spear game known as *jarid*, in which one horseman chases the other, and, when near enough, hurls a blunted wooden spear at the quarry. Gradually the groups began to gyrate more quickly ... rapid movements succeeded the slow. Every moment it became more like a real skirmish. Suddenly one party developed a charge – riding straight at the other. Somehow the "enemy" opened their ranks or avoided the clash of animals and accidents which seemed certain. This was the

Auda abu Tayi, a great tribal warrior. According to Lawrence he had been married 28 times and wounded 13 times before joining the Arab forces of the Emir Faysal. Then he ceremonially smashed his Turkish false teeth—and nearly starved until provided with an Allied set.

signal for a counter-attack and the development into full momentum of the fantasia. Rifle-bullets were now being fired every few seconds. The Princes were leading their men in a kind of wild, high-speed musical ride with magnificent judgment – all the more impressive because there was no carefully planned order. The dust of battle and smoke from home-made cartridges drifted across the field. Suddenly in front of us passed, at full gallop, a long sword held aloft before him, his hair and curls flying, and eyes alight with the pride which only young soldiers know, the Emir Faysal, the Viceroy of Mecca. His men came racing after him, their long curls streaming behind them, some of them half naked – for the Arab strips for battle – and all of them in the greatest excitement. The Crown Prince's party, equally soldierly, but keeping closer order, came galloping in to the attack. Wheeling at full speed in front of us, they charged down upon their "foe" and then, at the last moment, with admirable precision, were brought up all standing, the horses on their haunches.' No wonder that he remarks that the age of Ibn Saud was unique, combining as it did the picturesque life of the Middle Ages with the use of the creature comforts of the twentieth century.

We have seen that in 1865, when receiving Pelly, the Imam Faysal remarked that Riyadh was a strange place for a European to visit: we cannot even begin to picture his astonishment if, seventy years later, he had seen his grandson sitting down to dinner with the grand-daughter of Queen Victoria. In February 1938, Princess Alice accompanied her husband, the Earl of Athlone, brother of Queen Mary, on a journey across Arabia. Ibn Saud came to greet them at Jedda and gave a great feast, killing ten sheep for the thirty-four guests – the first time an Imam had ever sat to eat with a woman. *The Times* reported, 'After this Homeric repast the host regaled his guests with reminiscences of his romantic youth.' Princess Alice, in Arab robes and veil, her car followed by a mobile wireless transmitter, crossed Arabia from coast to coast as Sadlier had done with such discomfort a century before. Members of the British royal family in Riyadh provide a fitting climax to the account of travellers in Nejd.

Travellers in South-west Arabia

THERE WERE occasional references to Aden in the writings of travellers of the later Middle Ages. The Spanish Rabbi, Benjamin of Tudela, who may have sailed past en route from Basra to Egypt about 1170 referred to it as Eden or Middle India and thought that its mountains contained many independent tribes of Jews who lived by plundering their Muslim neighbours. Fifty years later Marco Polo said that its Sultan was one of the richest princes in the world, making a fortune through exporting horses to India. Nearby, he continued, there were two islands called Male and Female: the first populated entirely by men and the latter by women. Every spring the men would sail across the strait and dally for three months. Not far away was the island of Socotra where the people, Christians who wandered naked, were such skilful magicians that if any ship attempted to sail past without paying its dues, they could reverse the wind and bring it into harbour.

The battle between a 'leviathan' and a whale which Arnold von Harff claimed to have seen off Aden in 1496.

These tales were embroidered by the Rhinelander, Arnold von Harff, who asserted that he had visited the island about 1496 in a ship made without nails – magnetic rocks sucked out all pieces of iron. For good measure he added a great sea battle between a leviathan and a whale that he claimed to have witnessed. 'The leviathan had four feet with claws like a griffin and great broad fins like a bird, with which it leapt high out of the water. It had also a long thick tail, with which it struck fiercely, and a great mouth with huge teeth, so that with the long claws, the sharp teeth, the tail and the flying leaps, it attacked the whale with force and put it in great peril.' Just as things were looking black for it the whale sucked in three tons of water, and squirting it at its opponent, won by a knockout. As his Arabian experiences included a visit to the Prophet's tomb which he sited by the banks of a large river in Mecca and to a tribe of single-breasted Amazons – all achieved at jet-like speed – we must regretfully reject his testimony.

We come on to firmer ground in 1504 when the first Portuguese ship entered the Red Sea and two years later they established a castle on Socotra. In March 1513 the great Afonso d'Alboquerque anchored off Aden which he described as containing many beautiful houses under the shelter of a lofty range of mountains of which every peak was crowned by a castle. At dawn, bringing special ladders which held six men abreast, the Portuguese tried to storm the walls but the scaling ladders broke and the few who succeeded in penetrating were trapped. Realistically d'Alboquerque accepted defeat and, less realistically, set off in the hope of implementing two of his pet schemes: the first to land a force on the Arabian coast, raid Medina and carry off the body of the Prophet to exchange for the city of Jerusalem; and the other to divert the Nile into the Red Sea, thus literally leaving Cairo high and dry.

In 1538 a Turkish fleet arrived at Aden and, having courteously invited the Sultan aboard, hanged him from the yardarm. Shortly afterwards the whole area passed under Ottoman rule represented by a Pasha in Sanaa. It was to this official that two Iberian Jesuits, Fathers Pedro Paez and Antonio de Montserrat were sent after being captured off the Kuria Muria islands early in 1590. They had been ordered to go from Goa to Abyssinia, and in the turmoil caused by Turk and Portuguese battling for the mastery of the seas, decided that the easiest route would be through Basra and Aleppo to Cairo, and then down the Nile. Disguised as Armenians they reached Hormuz where they found a small Arab boat which promised to take them directly to Africa. They were betrayed, however, and became the first Europeans to see the Hadhramaut.

The Jesuits were entertained by the brother of the Sultan who gave them a drink, *gishr*, made from the rind of a fruit boiled in water: perhaps the first time that a drink made from the coffee plant was drunk by a westerner. They lived for some months among men who saturated their hair with butter and then curled it with hot irons and twice a day they had to endure a troop of women who wailed and beat their breasts in mourning for a princess. Finally they set out for Sanaa, riding non-stop for four days on camels and unable to doze for fear they should fall off. No other European entered the Yemen by this route until the 1930s. They remained for five years in the country, often working as gardeners, before they were ransomed. Father Paez eventually reached his goal where he was responsible for converting the Emperor to Catholicism, and, more enduringly, for some of the finest buildings in the country – the castles of Gondar – for which he made all the tools and trained all the carpenters, masons and labourers.

A century after the Portuguese, in April 1609, the first British ship arrived in the area. They were welcomed, according to John Jourdain, one of the merchants, by 'tabour and pipe and other heathen musicke' and lodged in a house which quickly became a prison. The Governor, a Greek renegade, suggested that they should unload their goods and, when some were landed, seized them as due to the Customs. The Governor was very 'discontenteous' that he could not acquire all their goods, but eventually agreed to release the ship, provided that Jourdain and another went to Sanaa as prisoners until all matters were settled. They arrived without mishap and were graciously received, being permitted to kiss the Pasha's vest. Jourdain asked permission to open a factory (trading post) in the country, 'whereunto hee awnswered that it could not bee permitted without expresse order from the Greate Turke, his master; and bringinge his order he would receive us with all his harte, putting it on his head'. Jourdain regained his ship at Mokha, which another member of the crew described as 'a City of great trading for our Commodities as Tynne, Iron, Lead, Cloth, Sword blades . . . It hath a great Bussart or Market every day in the weeke . . . an Oxe for 3 dollars, a Goat for half a dollar; as much fish for three pence as will suffice ten men for a meale.' In these happy circumstances, they successfully concluded their business. Jourdain had many more adventures before he was killed in a clash with the Dutch in the East Indies.

The year after Jourdain left Mokha, a second British trading fleet arrived there under the command of Sir Henry Middleton. The Greek renegade governor who had behaved so treacherously to their compatriots in Aden, welcomed the leaders ashore and soon showed that he had not lost his old touch. His men carried out an unexpected attack, killed eight of the Englishmen and put the rest in chains. Sir Henry was ordered to instruct the fleet to surrender and upon his refusal was thrown into 'a dirty Dog-kennel under a pair of Stairs . . . His Bed was no better than the hard Ground, and his Pillow a Stone. His Companions were Grief of Heart and a Multitude of Rats, which, if he chanced to fall asleep, soon awaked him with running over him.'

After a month, commands were received from the Pasha, and a miserable group had to march for a fortnight through the mountains where the ice was often a finger thick. They were welcomed by a band of 200 musicians but the Pasha 'with a frowning and angry countenance' told them that they must await, for their release, instruc-

The great fortress on Sirah island dominates the port of Aden. From a Dutch engraving of 1680.

165

tions from Constantinople. He did, however, disapprove of the conduct of the Governor of Mokha, offering 'to pull his Skin over his Ears and give you his Head' – a gift that, whatever his sentiments may have been, Sir Henry declined. After a further two months in prison, they were sent back to Mokha but were still held captive. Sir Henry managed to escape in a barrel and then, training his guns on the city, threatened to 'batter it about the Pasha's ears' if all looted goods were not at once restored and an indemnity paid. He further relieved his feelings with a little piracy and then sailed off to the Indies.

Middleton had been told that Christians could not be permitted access to any of the ports of the Holy Land of Arabia, but two years later the first Dutch fleet to arrive was made welcome. At Aden there was 'a terrible darkness, like a squall of rain, accompanied by a redness like a glowing oven, that was wonderful and dreadful to look at' – a sandstorm which left the ships covered with dust as thick as a thumb. The fleet then sailed eastwards to Shihr where they landed three of the party 'with a little cash and some Nuremburg wares of poor quality'. The King promised to protect them like the apple of his eye and they may well have enjoyed themselves among the local ladies 'who are very lascivious and have prettily shaped figures and limbs. Parents hold it a great honour whenever their daughters have knowledge of strangers.' It was some eighteen months later that the Admiral, Pieter van den Broecke returned, collected the two who survived and went on to Mokha. He was invited to Sanaa to meet the Pasha who kept great state with a suite of 200 richly dressed noblemen and a tame leopard. The Dutchman was greatly impressed by the antiquity of the city – admiring the well said to have been dug by Jacob in person which produced water too cold to drink, and seeing the relic of Noah's Ark kept in the Great Mosque.

The Pasha gave van den Broecke a coat of gold brocade but not permission to establish a factory in Mokha which he feared might become a springboard towards the Holy Cities. However, by 1620, both they and the English had resident merchants there and some survived the expulsion of the Turks in 1630. The Imam, now both temporal and spiritual leader of the country, was happy to make money out of trade – particularly in coffee – and there were often several European ships in the harbour. It was a Scot who bailed out the Niebuhr mission and later there was a resident renegade, one Campbell, who described himself as 'Captain-General of the Ordnance of the Kingdom of Senna'. He was a ship's gunner who had killed a fellow sailor in an argument, but a genial soul, always ready to welcome British passers by.

Few of the Europeans went far inland. An exception was a French mission at the beginning of the eighteenth century. Aden, rather surprisingly, reminded them of the Fair of St Germain, apart from its wonderful baths of marble and jasper. On their second visit to Mokha they were asked to send a surgeon to Muahib near Dhamar to treat the Imam who was suffering from an abscess in the ear. They found him an impressive figure for his eighty-seven years, simply dressed and keeping little pomp. He lodged them in his house and fed them from his own kitchen – an experience which Frenchmen naturally failed to appreciate. After three weeks the Imam pro-nounced himself cured and celebrated by marrying an eighteen-year-old girl to add to the 600 ladies that already graced his harem.

The number of travelling Englishmen increased rapidly as the eighteenth century ended. First there was the growing use of the overland route to India; then the need to forestall possible French action in the Napoleonic wars. Two visitors used words then rare but now familiar to us all. Major Rooke visited Mokha and was 'witness to a curious ceremony called in the East *champooing*; coming accidentally into the apartment of my friend, I beheld him stretched out quite naked on the floor, and prostrate on his face, while his attendants were rubbing him; I was at first apprehensive that the old fellow had fallen down in a fit, and thought that they were trying to bring him to life again; they laid hold of his flesh in different parts, pinching and clawing him with great violence'. Major Rooke was astonished to hear that this apparent torture was regarded as being pleasant but he was quite sure that it would never catch on in England. A few years later, in

1795, Professor Hugh Cleghorn of St Andrew saw the local fishermen sitting on a flat board called a *catamaran* and killing sharks from it. He was travelling on a secret service mission that few fiction writers could have imagined. The Dutch had recently joined in the war against Britain and their empire still included Ceylon, whose garrison consisted mainly of Swiss mercenaries. Cleghorn was going out to buy over these troops – a task in which he succeeded brilliantly and Ceylon changed masters with only token resistance.

Niebuhr had been fortunate enough during his brief stay to see the Imam leading the Friday devotions of the capital. Attended by princes and hundreds of soldiers he had ridden out, sheltered by a parasol – the emblem of royalty. On either side was borne a banner 'having upon it a small silver box filled with amulets, whose efficacy was imagined to render him invincible . . . the riders paced or galloped at pleasure, and all went in confusion. Near a gate were stationed some pairs of camels bearing carriages, in which some of the Imam's wives often ride upon such occasions: but the carriages were at this time empty, and only served to fill up the procession. Behind

The village and bay of Tamara on the island of Socotra, seen from the north in a lithograph of 1833.

the camels, which bore these, were 12 others, bearing nothing but some small flags, fixed, by way of ornament to their saddles.' Seventy years later in 1836 an official visitor, Mr Cruttenden of the Indian Navy watched the Friday ceremony. He wrote that the Imam carried a gold shafted spear, tipped with silver, and rode with his left hand resting on the shoulder of a confidential eunuch. Upon his arrival at the great open space in front of the palace, his attendants ranged themselves in a square, while, followed by his relatives, the Imam repeatedly charged around, feinting to attack the nearest horseman. He then dismounted and anyone who wished could kiss his knee and present a petition.

In the same year Sanaa saw one of the most extraordinary characters of the age. Joseph Wolff was born in 1795, the son of a German Rabbi and became an Anglican with a special mission to convert Oriental Jews. In 1821, followed by twenty camels loaded with Bibles, he began a tour which took him from Palestine to Baghdad and Shiraz, meeting on the way various Kurds who thrashed and stripped him. After a visit to the Caucasus he found himself in Alexandria, and, having engaged a servant who turned out to be an only partially reformed cannibal, set out for Bokhara. He accomplished the last part of the journey tied naked to a horse's tail. Leaving that city he had not gone far when he met a group, which having first threatened to turn him into sausages, contented itself with making him walk without clothes at the height of winter the 600 miles to Kabul where he was disappointed at not finding the lost tribes of Israel. He returned safely to England and was so hurt at finding himself regarded as the re-incarnation of Baron Munchausen that he left quickly on another missionary enterprise. In 1836 he went to Abyssinia, causing some confusion by being taken for the Coptic Patriarch in disguise, and from there he went to the Yemen in pursuit of the Rechabites – a nomadic tribe of teetotal Jews mentioned by Jeremiah. The local Jews turned out in fact to be urban artisans, and despite giving them copies of *Robinson Crusoe* in Arabic, he had little success with them. This was partly due to the fact that although he claimed to know nearly every

Oriental language, no one could understand a word that he said in any of them. On his way back to the coast he encountered a fanatical tribe, which like so many others in the Middle East, felt that he merited a sound flogging. He then spent what must have been for him a comparatively quiet time as a curate in Massachusets but soon returned to England. Not long afterwards he was asked to go to Bokhara to ascertain the fate of two British officers who had been imprisoned by the Emir. Styling himself 'The Grand Dervish of England, Scotland, Ireland and the whole of Europe and America', he travelled in a shovel hat, a doctor's scarlet hood and an academic gown. Unfortunately he arrived too late to help the captives but did for once manage to return to England with a whole skin. He ended his days as a country vicar in Somerset.

Although commercially coffee is picked from bushes, the tree in its wild state can grow more than thirty feet tall. From an engraving of 1680.

A man of similar background but of far less flamboyant personality followed Wolff into Sanaa twenty years later. The Rev Henry Aaron Stern was also a German-born Jew attempting to convert former co-religionists to the Church of England. He had a long period of service in Baghdad and Persia before following the Army into the Crimea to try his luck on the Russian Jews. When this failed he went to the Yemen where he transformed himself into the Dervish, Abdallah, shaved his beard, head and moustache and went up to Sanaa. He stayed some months but despite a favourable reception, failed to win any lasting converts. Then he crossed the Red Sea and moved as a missionary among the mysterious Falasha, the so-called Black Jews of Ethiopia. He clashed with the half-crazed Emperor Theodore, who according to Stern's biographer challenged him 'Rogue! Villain! Knave. If you are not a woman will you make the choice of a weapon – sword, spear, pistol, or even cannon and fight me?'

'Without manifesting either fear or contempt', the Reverend Mr Stern refused, whereupon two of the men guarding him had fits. Stern was then imprisoned in the famous fortress of Magdala where he remained for four years before being rescued by the expedition under General Napier. He passed the rest of his life in the less hazardous but scarcely more rewarding task of attempting to convert the Jews of Whitechapel.

Two adventurous Frenchmen explored the Yemen in the middle of the century. Arnaud had been a pharmacist with an Egyptian regiment before serving the Imam in the same capacity. In 1843 he returned to Sanaa but his real target was Marib – the ancient capital of one of the great pre-Islamic realms. A sophisticated society had grown up around an enormous dam, reputedly built by the Queen of Sheba, which brought prosperity to a large area. The collapse of this dam, probably in the sixth century, had been a traumatic event which had transformed both the history and the geography of the Peninsula and it had left ruins which are still visible. Arnaud, dressed in a shirt to his knees on top of pants to mid-calf, a turban and sandals, attached himself to one of the camel trains which regularly took corn to the East and returned laden with salt. They were stopped several times by blackmailing tribesmen but eventually they reached a plain incredibly rich in pre-Islamic tombs and inscriptions. He was told how a white man, saying that he was from the farthest west, had arrived ten years before 'to read the stones' and, receiving a letter no man knew how, had mysteriously vanished, leaving a tip of antique gold pieces. It was suspected that Arnaud was also a magician seeking treasure and more than once his life was in danger. After a few days among the ruins he caught the returning caravan and doubtless thought himself fortunate to arrive back in Sanaa without mishap.

In 1869 Joseph Halévy arrived in the Yemen on a mission for the Académie des Inscriptions of Paris. He moved around in local Jewish costume with long ringlets, in an old ragged cotton burnous without shoes or pants, but giving out that he was a learned Rabbi from Jerusalem. The prestige of belonging to the sacred city enabled him to threaten tormentors with a painful doom if they molested him too far: but it led some of the less educated Jews to take him for the Messiah, while some of the more backward Arabs debated whether he were the Mahdi who was expected to save the world, or the Anti-Christ who would come to destroy it. Once he was asked about the great invisible stone which was believed to be descending slowly over Jerusalem and which will end the world when it touches the highest minaret: tactfully he replied that only holier men than himself could see it.

He travelled in the utmost discomfort. As a Jew he was not allowed to ride a donkey in the presence of Muslims unless he were ill, which he often was: any Muslim was entitled to inspect him to see that he was not shamming. He was warned not to go far from Sanaa because of the dangers from both devils and tribesmen but on occasions he was very kindly received. Once, however, he was startled when his hostess removed her voluminous trousers and washed them in the dish from which they had just eaten. He became the first European since Roman times to enter Najran and he returned through Marib bringing back a total of 685 inscriptions which greatly increased knowledge of pre-Islamic Arabia.

In 1849 the Turks re-established a rather feeble presence on the coast of the Yemen but the opening of the Suez Canal enabled them to send reinforcements. In April 1871 they reoccupied Sanaa, almost welcomed as putting an end to a worse than usual period of anarchy. With a short break they were there until 1919 so our next three travellers were to come while they were still in control. The Ottomans were, however, plagued with rebellions which made them discourage tourists. It was a period of some material progress and bicycles, cafes and shops with somewhat dusty European goods made their appearance in the capital.

Walter Harris came in 1892. He had already lived in Morocco where he became known as a master of disguise, penetrating where no European would have been safe, so that bluffing his way across the Aden frontier in the character of a Greek merchant must have been child's play for him. He was delighted by the change of scenery: 'We had entered Arabia Felix! On all sides of us were tiny streams, splashing and tumbling through fern-covered banks over pebbles and stones. One does not realize what music there is in the sound of running water until one has travelled over deserts where the muddy pools are two or three days apart.' However, as usual in such a paradise, man was vile and a party of forty lay in wait to plunder his small caravan. A friendly stranger warned them and led them over a precipitous track to avoid the ambushers.

Upon his arrival in Sanaa, Harris triumphantly waved his British passport – which promptly led to his imprisonment as a spy. He remained in jail for five days and was then allowed to wander around the city. He saw the ruins of the great palace-temple of Ghumdan: 1600 steps had led up to a tower seven storeys high, each smaller than the one below until the floor of the topmost was a single sheet of marble. At each corner of the roof was a stone lion through whose open mouth the wind made roaring sounds like the king of beasts.

He then made his way down to the sea, amazed as are all who go that way, by the countryside around Manakha. 'Wonderful, stupendous it was! Around us on all sides the bare fantastic peaks and perpendicular precipices, on the edge of one of which we perched, and up the face of which we could see the path we had climbed winding in and out. Below us, far below like little ants, we could see our mules and men toiling up . . . Of all the places that it has ever been my lot to see, Manakha is the most wonderfully situated. The town is perched on a narrow strip of mountain that joins two distinct ranges and it forms the watershed of two great valleys . . . the walls of the houses seem to hang over the precipices and one can look down into the two great valleys at the same time. Curious and wonderful as this is, the grand effect of the scene is doubly increased by the extraordinary peaks which rise above the place – enormous pinnacles . . . Great bare rocky crags, perpendicular and ending like sugar

A view of Mokha about 1830 shows the Arab houses inside the walls and the African huts outside.

173

loafs.' Harris returned to Morocco where he both made history – he was kidnapped by a celebrated bandit, an 'incident' which became international – and recorded it for *The Times*. He was a cheerful fellow who amused all with whom he came into contact from kings to cameleers and his books are as lively as his personality.

In 1905 two men in their early twenties met in the House of Commons and decided to go to Sanaa. One, Leland Buxton, had been a member of the party which impersonated the Sultan of Zanzibar and received an official welcome at Cambridge from both the Vice-Chancellor and the Mayor. Later he had been active in Bulgaria, fighting with guerilla bands against the Turks. The other, the Hon. Aubrey Herbert also knew the Balkans well and was later said to be the model for John Buchan's hero Sandy Arbuthnot. They were greeted in Hodeidah by the sight of an aged criminal who had been fettered to the ground for forty years: all, including the victim, had forgotten the reason for this punishment but he remained there despite the strong suspicion that he was really a slightly eccentric saint. Later they were shipwrecked off Bahrain and Herbert's attempt to cross Arabia by land was frustrated by illness and official obstruction.

A charming picture of an Arabian child in holiday clothes by Henry Salt made during his visit to Mokha in 1809.

Subsequently Herbert became an MP and used to make his speeches from brief notes in Turkish. The war found them both in the Arab Bureau in Cairo before Herbert was sent with Lawrence on the extraordinary attempt to bribe the Turkish General surrounding Kut to raise the siege. Buxton had the scarcely less hazardous task of representing the government in Ethiopia at a time of civil war. Herbert later, possibly with regret, refused an invitation to become the first king of Albania.

One of the last pre-war visitors to the Yemen was Hugh Scott, an entomologist from the British Museum. In 1938 he saw the old Imam, who had then been in power for more than thirty years, going to the Friday prayer as his ancestors had done. He was in a huge old four-wheeled carriage, with an attendant walking beside it whirling a great umbrella while a bodyguard danced, waved their daggers and shrieked out patriotic songs. An empty car followed in case of necessity. They were received in audience by the Imam, who squatted on the floor counting the silver coins which were all the contents of the Treasury. Petitions were constantly brought in, including one for permission to leave the army from a soldier who had been killed in action: the Imam solemnly approved it by dipping his finger in a bowl of red ochre and running it along the text.

Aden and its hinterland

Aden, by the nineteenth century, had greatly declined from the great estate of the past and a visitor in 1809 thought it a 'wretched heap of ruins and miserable huts, which none, except the lowest Arabs, would think of inhabiting. The natives appear squalid and unhealthy, and the lower classes are as depraved in their habits as those in most Arabian towns. Among the ruins some fine remains of ancient splendour are to be met with, which form a melancholy contrast to the general desolation of the scene.' A report a few years later put the population at 800, living among 'a few minarets tottering to their fall'.

This unprepossessing place was occupied by the Indian Navy with little bloodshed in January 1839. The conqueror, Captain Haines, thought little of the folk that he was to rule for fifteen years. 'Their youth is spent,' he wrote, 'in the study of dissimulation and intrigue and their older age in practicing these vices.' Haines laboured to make the port into the entrepôt which it was destined to become, but his interest in the hinterland was limited to the immediate aim of preventing attacks by hostile tribesmen. The reception of one of the first parties to go far inland from the base, that of Colonel Miles in 1870, did not encourage further visitors. Beduins threatened to hang the next Christians to come into their area, and Miles found universal poverty – even a Sultan had a single slave, no furniture and no power beyond a musket-shot of his dreary hovel. The women were coarse and ugly.

It was not until the beginning of this century that a serious attempt was made to explore the interior of south Arabia. The man concerned was Wyman Bury, an army officer who had fought with Moroccan rebels in 1895. He adopted the name of Abdullah Mansur and lay for hours on the rocks until he felt himself sufficiently brown to pass for an Arab. Then in the fashion of the local warriors he rubbed indigo into his skin. Tribesmen, when freshly anointed, shine an amazing metallic blue, wearing nothing but a loin cloth held up by a cartridge belt in which is stuck a curving dagger as richly adorned as its owner can afford. Some have gold coins, apparently of Byzantine origin, adorning the hilt while the scabbard bulges with semi-precious stones. The indigo rubs off very easily and the present writer has had a very blue hand after greeting a group and it wears off, too, on the white beards of the elders as they stroke them philosophically. Every man of tribal birth carried a fire-arm even if, as one still saw in the 1950s, it dated from the Franco-Prussian war or even earlier.

At his first halt a girl brought Bury some coffee and courteously enquired if it tasted all right. 'Auntie fell down the well yesterday,' she explained, 'and father has gone off to cut some grappling sticks.' This is a not uncommon event in the area and the writer's opinion was once sought as to what should be done about an old woman who, months after being pulled up from a well, still 'felt poorly' whenever it was suggested that she might walk five miles to get some firewood or spend a scorching day looking after the goats.

Bury saw many places where no European had ever been. He wrote of the tribesmen: 'the lowest type,

Freya Stark, after one of her journeys to Hadhramaut, returned to Aden by dhow. The voyage from Bal Haf to Shuqra, 100 miles, cost three rupees and took a day and a half. By road it would have taken ten days.

A photograph by Hugh Scott of a *mafraj* where a Yemeni gentleman entertains his friends. The small window panes are often of alabaster, or coloured glass.

indigent, churlish, treacherous and grasping – a pariah preying on the weak and filching from the strong . . . Still, with all his faults, he can die like a lone wolf when his time comes. His gamut of emotion is a simple octave, religion at one end and avarice at the other, the latter an absorbing passion which influences most of his deliberate acts and thoughts.' Several times Bury was ambushed and fifty years later this writer met an old man who claimed to have shot at him. His wanderings took him to a tribe which had been decimated by smallpox, and which, as he delicately put it, 'had suspended the marriage laws in favour of all guests of fighting stock'. Another tribe made a palm toddy which laid them out for days. He visited Yashbum, where the shaikhs were the direct descendants of those who had led the resistance to the Roman invasion of 24 BC and so were one of the oldest dynasties in the world. He was also probably the first Englishman to spend his honeymoon in Sanaa.

Another period of thirty years elapsed during which there was no serious attempt to learn much about the areas north and east of Aden. R. A. B. Hamilton, later Lord Belhaven, spent much of the 1930s walking, often with a single companion, throughout the Western Aden Protectorate of which we may regard him as the last of the explorers. He marched from the coast up through the wild Arqub Pass 'where you feel like an ant climbing over the cinders of a boiler-room . . . Cast here and there as if by a giant's spade, stand cone-shaped hills of red and grey volcanic slag.' He attended a feast at which his host politely 'stood in the background, occasionally taking as a snack a half-pound slab of meat, fat-girdled, putting all he could into his very capacious jaws, and cutting off the residue with his dagger close to his lips . . . chewed with open mouth, while the fat and gravy ran through his beard and down the outside of his hairy throat on to his unclean smock'. It has often been noticed that south Arabians have meat so rarely that when it is available they tend to forget their table manners.

'Ham' enjoyed the company of the Arabs, whose easy charm often made an Englishman feel that he has been accepted 'but this can never be so: he is white, they are

brown; he is a Christian, they are Muslims: he is European, they are Asiatic. Between him and the Arabs is an unbridgable gulf. He can never be one of them in their eyes.' There is the same note of sadness in his description of the land itself: 'Arabia is a hard barren mistress and those who serve her she pays in weariness, sickness of the body and distress of mind.' Yet he hardly exaggerates the sentiments of many who lived and served in the area when he concluded 'Not a day will pass in all your life but you will remember some facet of that opal-land, not a night will pass without some twist of dream.'

Limitless sand and a merciless sky. The aspect of the Rub al-Khali—the Empty Quarter.

Hadhramaut
North-east of Aden lies the Wadi Hadhramaut running from almost the edge of the Empty Quarter down to the

sea at Sayhut. It was a name known to earliest antiquity, occurring in Genesis where the name has been interpreted as meaning 'the valley of the presence of death'. Herodotus described how flying snakes guarded the source of its wealth – myrrh and incense. The incense tree has an ash-coloured trunk with branches starting near the ground. Cuts are made in the stem and a green transparent gum comes out, hardening after a few days. Then, scraped off, it was carried on the legendary route through the great cities of Shabwa, Marib and Mecca until it burned on the altars of Memphis or Jerusalem. The commodity was so precious that Pliny believed that any porter who strayed from the road was punished by death.

Much of the spiritual life of the area centred around the shrine of the 'Patron Saint' – the Prophet Hud who was believed to be the Biblical Eber, great-great grandson of Noah. Pursued by his enemies he had vanished into a cleft in the mountains while his faithful camel had to remain outside, transformed into a great stone that is visible to this day. The tomb provided an oasis of security which the most violent foes never dreamed of violating: so sacred was it that a stick or stone removed would come alive, leaping and screaming until it was replaced.

A thousand years ago, a descendant of the Prophet, Sayyid Ahmad ibn Isa settled in the Wadi and by preaching and by force overcame both pagans and heretical Muslims. His descendants multiplied and came to dominate the area as a spiritual aristocracy. However there was little enough in the scattered oases to support them and their tribal followers, so large numbers had to go abroad to seek their living. Some went to Zanzibar but many more to the East Indies where it was reckoned that there were 80,000 living in 1931. Many of them married before they set sail but their wives never left the Hadhramaut. Often they raised second families abroad but then they would return, perhaps after thirty years, to reclaim their first brides. Many made great fortunes as merchants or hoteliers in Singapore or Batavia but even if they returned as millionaires, they would resume their old tribal feuds or pay exorbitant sums for the little agricultural land available.

This unique civilization was scarcely known to the West before the beginning of the present century. The first traveller to leave any description was a Bavarian soldier who had served in the Greek Army: Baron Adolf von Wrede who landed at Mukalla in 1843, passing under the name of Abd al-Hud. Some of the people realized that he was a European and plied him with questions as to the number of eunuchs at the court of Queen Victoria, and whether it was true that the Czar had a bodyguard of 700 cannibals and was himself seven yards tall with a single eye in the middle of his forehead. Amongst these people with such a limited knowledge of Europe he found a shaikh who was reading Walter Scott's *Life of Napoleon Buonaparte*. He described astonishing quicksands named the Bahr (Sea) of Saffi after a king whose army had perished there. 'A melancholy scene presented itself to my astonished sight! Conceive an immense sandy plain strewed with numberless undulating hills, which gave it the impression of a moving sea. Not a single trace of vegetation, be it ever so scanty, appears to animate the

Throughout recorded history incense has been used in religious ceremonies. As it grows mainly on the south coast of Arabia this region became immensely rich through the incense trade. From a drawing of 1575.

vast expanse. Not a single bird interrupts with its note the calm of death, which rests upon this tomb of the Sabean army.' His Beduin guides said that vast treasures were guarded in its depths by ghosts and they refused to accompany him as he crept forward to hurl a plumb line which rapidly sank more than 60 fathoms. Alas for a picturesque tale, no one else has ever seen these voracious sands, not even Philby who drove a large car over the exact area where they were supposed to be without noticing them!

Some days later Wrede arrived at the little town of Sif, just as the people prepared to celebrate a religious festival. The Arabs were nervous, for it was only four years since the British had taken Aden and recently crops had failed since two Naval officers had copied Himyaritic inscriptions near the coast. Wrede was taken for an English spy, and the people 'raised a horrible cry' and demanded that he should be put to death. He was dragged, covered with blood and dust, before the Sultan but was saved by the intercession of his guides. The Sultan contented himself with looting his luggage and confiscating his notes. It is not clear what happened to Wrede after his return to Europe: one writer has it that he joined the Turkish Army and another that he emigrated to Texas.

It was fifty years before another European entered the country and once again it was a German, Leo Hirsch, an Arabic and Himyaritic scholar of repute. Although he travelled in local costume, he admitted that he was a Westerner who had come to study Islam. He became the first European to reach the Wadi Hadhramaut where he was so well received that the Sultan wrote a poem in his praise. He went on to Tarim where there lived the largest community of Sayyids. One was prepared to entertain him but a fanatical mob gathered and threatened to burn down the house. His account of the journey is exactly what one might expect from a deeply learned Teuton.

The same year, 1893, the Hadhramaut saw its first Englishwoman. Mabel Bent had accompanied her husband Theodore on many previous journeys, including one to Bahrain (which they regarded as the original home of the Phoenicians), and they had been the first to measure the ruins of Zimbabwe, which they regarded as the work of Arabs. They knew little Arabic and travelled with all European comforts including an Indian surveyor, a botanist from Kew, a Greek servant and an Egyptian naturalist. They produced the first popular book on the Hadhramaut and Mrs Bent took the first photographs.

They noticed how many of the Hadhrami towns looked like Rhenish castles of mud. Their escorts were 'tiny spare men, quite beardless, with very refined gentle faces; they might easily have been taken for women, so gentle and pretty were they'. The girls, however, were 'grotesque beyond description' for they dyed their faces bright yellow with tumeric and had black stripes, red noses and green spots on their cheeks. Even worse than painting their faces, they were 'bold hussies' who peered into the tents where anyway the visitors got little rest for all night the Beduins were 'yelling, bawling, singing and screeching'. The Bents were interested in the local cures, observing the habit of branding with a hot iron for most pains and they recorded the tale of a man, who for a bet, ate all the fat from a goat. When, perhaps not surprisingly, he suffered from stomach ache, a local sage lit a fire around him to remelt the fat.

The Bents, partly through their own standoffishness, were not welcomed. At Shibam there were prayers that the land might be spared the presence of unbelievers. They concluded 'religion and fanaticism are together so deeply engrained in the Hadhramaut, that anything like friendly intercourse with the people is at present next to impossible ... Religion is the moving spirit of the place; without it the whole Hadhramaut would have been abandoned long ago as useless, but the inhabitants regard it as the most sacred spot on earth.'

Another forty years were to elapse before serious explorers again set foot in the Wadi. This time the party consisted of the Dutch Consul from Jedda, van der Meulen, and a German geographer, Hermann von Wissmann. Their journey started by car because their escorting camelmen were at feud with the tribesmen immediately outside Mukalla. They paused to admire the famous

George Wyman Bury (1874–1920) was the first European to see much of what later became the Western Aden Protectorate. Who's Who gave his hobbies as 'Psychical Research and pistol shooting'. A strong individualist, he had numerous quarrels with the British Government.

local tobacco which gets its distinctive flavour from being three times manured – once with bird droppings, then with rotten fish and finally with a mixture of human and animal dung. Like all travellers they were amazed at the first sight of Wadi Duan: after crossing an apparently endless flat gravelly plain, there suddenly yawns a chasm 1000 feet deep in the midst of which is 'a forgotten bit of paradise waiting for the Day of Judgement'. Ingrams later described the same thrilling view: 'At first we saw no houses; then out of the pale brown sandy cliffs appeared great castles, so harmonizing with their background as to be invisible at first sight, huddling at the foot of the opposite cliff as though they wanted to climb the wall.'

Wissmann and van der Meulen went on to Shibam, which reminded them of a chocolate cake covered with sugar, and completed their journey in motor cars which had been brought up from the coast on the backs of camels and assembled in the Wadi. Like all comers they noticed the extraordinary difference between the three principal

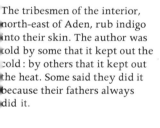

The tribesmen of the interior, north-east of Aden, rub indigo into their skin. The author was told by some that it kept out the cold: by others that it kept out the heat. Some said they did it because their fathers always did it.

towns of the Hadhramaut. Shibam has towering houses, pressed close together for defence, Saiyun has fine mosques and houses while Tarim consists of great modern palaces of often hideous design and glaring colours. They are paid for by money from Java and it is difficult to realize that they are built of dried mud and straw, with lime plaster polished with smooth flints until it shines like marble. Even the huge slender minaret is of mud.

They tried to return overland to Aden but were ambushed on the way. Van der Meulen does not say whether he was a fan of cowboy films but perhaps he was: he put his solar topee on a rock and while the bandits were firing at it, he and his companion slipped away.

Not long afterwards another German, Hans Helfritz, arrived. He was a magnificent photographer but otherwise seems to have lacked the gifts of an explorer. Indeed, as Freya Stark tartly remarked, 'he seemed to have got himself threatened with shooting and death more often than was reasonable for the most tactless tourist' and

A Hadrami girl dressed for a festival. Her face would be painted yellow with spots of green.

The great Wadi Hadhramaut is as dramatic as the Grand Canyon.

overleaf
The storming of Shinas during the British campaign against the pirates of Ras al-Khaimah in 1810. This was the first of three campaigns—a treaty was not concluded until ten years later.

indeed on nearly every page he is in danger. This reached a peak when, after a quarrel over donkeys 'it was no pleasant sensation to have an oil-smeared dagger within reach of one's throat, or to feel the point of a rifle against one's chest . . . Fortunately several Beduin women happened to come along, and laughed heartily at what seemed to them a highly comic situation'. It says much for the tolerance of the Arabs that this absurd character managed to be the first European into Shabwa (which he left after a few moments under a hail of stones), and to be the first since the sixteenth-century Jesuits to enter Yemen from the east. After two terms in jail, he was invited to leave the country as soon as possible.

During his visit to the Hadhramaut van der Meulen was asked by many of the local people to request Aden to establish a British presence in the Wadi. Insecurity was making life almost impossible: tribesmen engaged in family feuds could not leave their houses because their relatives sat with rifles aimed at the doors, while in every cultivated area, warriors had to guard the crops night and day. Late in 1934, pressed by a statesmanlike millionaire, Sayyid Bubakr al-Kaf, who was building a motor road up from the coast out of his own pocket, the Government sent an official, Harold Ingrams, to report. Accompanied by his wife Doreen, whose role was to be almost as important as his own, he did a nine-week reconnaissance by donkey to Duan and the Wadi and then by camel to the sea at Sayhut where they found the tomb of a saint with a large tree pushing through the dome. According to legend, he had been born with a small shrub growing out of his head but during his life had kept it pruned.

The Ingrams returned in 1936, and, helped by Sayyid Bubakr, established the famous Peace which enabled the Wadi to enjoy a period of tranquillity. Ingrams described how the passion for agreements spread among the inhabitants: the Sayyids of Shihr made a treaty that none of them would allow their wives to spend more than ten dollars on a dress or more than two on a tea party. The people went unarmed and in security; the road from Mukalla and, finally, flights from Aden Airways, transformed visits to the Hadhramaut from travel to tourism.

One last traveller is worthy of record. Freya Stark made numerous friends of both sexes and described how a girl first knew that she was to be married when her relatives arrived to varnish her face yellow and paint her hands and feet. All the third day of the celebration she sat under a red veil until her husband, whom she now saw for the first time, arrived. When some of Miss Stark's rings were stolen, a Sayyid wrote a talisman that the suspects would have to drink: before the ordeal the property was mysteriously restored. Finally she had a bout of measles

and only just managed to prevent well-wishers from branding her neck with hot irons. The RAF evacuated her to Aden, to resume a career which led her to create a political party in Egypt and to further travels which are always described with interest and elegance.

Socotra

As we have already seen, the Portuguese built a fort on the island but their presence lasted only a few years. The inhabitants continued to regard themselves as Christians although in the next century a visiting priest thought their rites distinctly odd. They had churches of which they daily anointed the altar with butter, they abominated wine and pork and sacrificed to the Moon. If no rains appeared they appointed a priest as a victim and after giving an ultimatum to the Moon, cut off his hands if there was no immediate flood.

The island was under the control of the Mahra Sultan of Qishn and seems to have attracted little attention until the British authorities, in the 1830s, considered its use as a coaling station. Two officers, Wellsted and Cruttenden, whom we have already met in the Yemen, spent two months early in 1834 surveying the land. Wellsted reported that the inhabitants 'were shown the various articles in our tent, to the use of which they were as utter strangers as the veriest savage in the wilds of New Zealand'. They did not even know the use of money and trade was conducted by bartering ghee. He gave a giggling Beduin lady a pair of trousers which she proceeded to don: doubtless an advantage for he thought that the girls, although otherwise comely enough, had the thickest legs that he had ever seen.

Many of the people lived in caves surrounded by low stone walls which served as a fold for their abundant cattle. Their only furniture was a stone for grinding corn, some skins on which to sleep or to hold water, and some earthen cooking pots. Often a rough cloth hanging from four pegs served as a cradle when one was needed. Fleas were everywhere.

The island was so isolated that none of the people had ever seen a dog and they thought that the black face of a

These tall straw hats are worn by the peasant women of Hadhramaut when they work in the fields.

Nubian servant must be that of Satan in person. Their method of justice was simple: a suspect was tied on a hill top and if rain fell on him within three days, he was considered guilty and stoned to death. The scenery was superb; 'It has been my good fortune,' wrote Wellsted, 'to have traversed much of the East, and to have witnessed every variety which has been there assumed by nature. That of Socotra yields to none in wildness and romantic grandeur.' The effect was increased by its unique vegetation, for between 800 and 2000 feet grows the extraordinary Dragon's Blood Tree which exuded a dark crimson gum. It stands some twenty feet high with numerous short branches thickly intertwined and covered with foot-long leaves spread out like fans.

Some months later, Haines was sent to buy the island for about £2000 from the Sultan whom he found old, blind, deformed and attired in rags. Despite his penury he refused to sell an inch of land, saying that 'It was a gift of the Almighty to the Mahras, and has descended from our forefathers to their children.' Disappointed though he was, Haines could not but admire the Sultan's integrity. Subsequently a British force landed but withdrew after a few months, decimated by fever.

In 1896 the Bents spent a few weeks there. They resurrected a tale of Socotran magic – a man had recently eloped with a girl from the mainland by turning her into a seal. She swam to the island and resumed her proper shape. We have seen their interest in medicine, so they must have enjoyed the occasion when the village doctor treated their servant 'by making several slashes on the top of his head and cupping him with a horn, which he sucked, and having spent a little time blowing in different directions, settled down, crouching over the patient . . . muttering a few words alternately with spitting, slightly and often in his face'. The cure was practically instantaneous.

Like other visitors, the Bents thought that the people of Socotra, with their distinctive language, were an aboriginal people who existed before the Arabs entered the area. This is, however, still a mystery for Socotra remains one of the least known areas of the Middle East.

Travellers in Oman

THE GULF is probably the oldest seaway in the world and many archaeologists believe that it was upon its waters that mankind first learned to navigate. The fleet of Alexander the Great sailed there and later it provided the route along which Sindbad the Sailor set out in search of profit but more frequently found adventure. The entrance to the Gulf is dominated by Muscat which is, with the exception of Aden, the finest natural harbour in Arabia. It is, wrote Lord Curzon, 'probably one of the most picturesque places in the world. From a distance immense granitic masses of rock, with jagged outline of cliff and crag, are seen ascending in gloomy abruptness from the sea. Far inland ridge rises upon ridge, splintered edge above and savage fissures between, the impression being that of a country upheaved from nature's primaeval cauldron, and still scarred and blackened by those terrific fires ... On a tiny patch of ground Muscat lies, its plastered houses glittering against the sombre background like a seagull's wing against an angry sky.'

Little was known of Muscat in the West before the great Afonso d'Alboquerque arrived in 1507 to demand its submission to his sovereign, Manoel of Portugal. The inhabitants were not prepared to die in the cause of their overlord, the King of Hormuz, and submitted with reasonable grace. A hostile force, however, seemed to be gathering and d'Alboquerque, never a man to shrink from a fight, stormed the city and set it on fire. There were so many prisoners that the Portuguese cut off the noses and ears of those that they did not need and turned them loose. Divine approval of this pious practice of Holy War was attested by a miracle: the mosque fell on top of the men who were cutting away its supports but they emerged unscathed.

Despite brief setbacks, the Portuguese were to rule there for a century and a half. They built the great forts of Jilali and Marani which still loom over the harbour. They made no attempt to expand their dominion inland or to convert the local people, scarcely interfering in their domestic affairs.

Portuguese rule in Muscat was prolonged through the disunity of the people of the hinterland. The inhabitants of Inner Oman belong to the Ibadhi sect which is regarded as heretical by most other Muslims. They do not believe that their leader, or Imam, need be a descendant of the Prophet but that they should chose the best of the community as their spiritual and temporal head: an idea doubtless admirable in theory but in practice likely to cause disputes. The Imam was absolute until he broke a religious law or, worse still, introduced an innovation when it became the duty of all good men to oppose him: this, of course, was another recipe for chaos. However in 1625 a member of the Yaaribah tribe became Imam and proceeded to make his power first effective and then hereditary.

It is told that when in 1649 his successor politely requested to be allowed to buy provisions in Muscat *suq*, the Portuguese Commandant sent him a pork chop as a deliberate insult. Some time later the Commandant was believed to have designs upon the daughter of a wealthy Indian merchant, who resolved to betray the city to save his girl. He sent a message to the Imam that, as good Christians, the Portuguese celebrated Sundays by getting drunk; then he opened the gates when they were in no position to defend themselves.

The expulsion of the Portuguese provided opportunities for their rivals, the English and the Dutch and travellers' tales become more frequent. Nearly all strain the imagination in their attempt to convey the heat of Muscat. None seem to have outbid the fifteenth-century Persian who described how the plains were covered in roasted gazelles while roasted fowls fell out of the air and boiled fish might be scooped from the sea. Many told of eggs or fish frying on the rocks or of thermometers bursting but in the rich English of the Restoration John Fryer wrote: 'At night we saw Muscat, whose vast and horrid Mountains no Shade but Heaven does hide, though they cover the City with a horrid one; reflecting thence the Heat scorching us at Sunsetting, and aboard ship; within their fiery Bosom the Pilots find secure Harbour for their weather-beaten ships.' A few years later a Dutchman wrote of 'boiling cauldron or sweating tubs' and how his friends used to leap into the sea to pass the day there. A nineteenth-century sailor summed up the matter: 'There is only a sheet of brown paper between here and Hell.'

A more favourable picture of Muscat was given by the Rev Mr Ovington, who published an account in 1689. A few lines of preface by the Poet Laureate, Nahum Tate, deserve to be rescued from oblivion:

. . . Thanks are due
From Britain's Sons, Industrious Friend to you,
Fame shall in State your usefull Book Install
In Bodley's Pile, the Muses' Capitol.

Ovington remarked upon 'the Temperance and Justice of the Arabians of Muscat, for which Two things they are more remarkable than any other Natives this day in the World'. No one, he said, was more rigidly abstemious and even tea and coffee were 'abominated as Bug-bear Liquors. He that would turn Advocate for any of these sorts of Drink, and to commend the Use of them as convenient for their Stomachs, as fit to chear their Hearts, and chase away Melancholy from their Spirits would be looked upon as a vile Contemner of their Law, and an Encourager of Libertinism and Intemperance.' Furthermore, 'the Inferiours are freed from the violence of all Splenitick Disgusts, and unreasonable Severities of their Superiours. A Revengeful Master cannot vent his Passion at his Pleasure upon his Servant, nor an unnatural Parent Beat and Chastise his son at his Will.' Even the Government was averse to shedding blood and the rare criminal was immured and 'leasurely dies between Two Walls'.

This picture, published in 1680, does not exaggerate the amount of maritime activity in the thriving harbour of Muscat at the time.

MASKATE

195

It is an attractive picture and one is saddened to learn from the next writer, Captain Alexander Hamilton, that Mr Ovington never went anywhere near Muscat but got all his information second-hand in India. However, Hamilton did admit that the Muscatis were remarkable for their 'Humility and Urbanity'. Most later writers confirm this except for one surly old sailor who, ordered to write an account of their manners and customs could only, after deep cogitation come up with 'As to manners they have none and their customs are beastly.' Later writers

The two great Portuguese forts dominating Muscat, pictured in pencil and watercolour by William Daniell in 1793. R. G. Searight, Esq, London.

comment also upon their honesty, upon the huge quantities of goods that lay unattended in the streets but were never pilfered.

In the 1720s and 1730s the country was torn by civil wars which led to an occupation by the Persians. This lasted until 1744 when a local Governor, Ahmad ibn Said, invited the garrison to a banquet and slaughtered them as they ate. Having thus proved himself a sound patriot and the best of the Muslims, he was recognized as Imam and his dynasty rules to this day.

Netting sprats in the Trucial States. When fish is plentiful it is also fed to cattle or used for manure.

Under Ahmad's forceful rule the country achieved stability, and links with Europe multiplied. Europe meant mostly England and its dependency, India. The links with India had always been strong for Oman is almost an island with the sea on three sides and the deserts of the Empty Quarter taking up most of the fourth. It looked, therefore, upon the Persians and the Baluchis as nearer neighbours than most of the other Arabs. Necessity had turned the Omanis into the finest sailors of all the area and Muscat served as the entrepôt for nearly all the trade of the Gulf.

Visits from the Royal Navy became frequent and one of the earliest was by HMS *Seahorse* in 1775, when Midshipman Horatio Nelson was among her officers. The custom grew that each crew should paint its name on the rocks above the town and so a record has been preserved. Relations were cemented by a Treaty of 1800, the first between a European Power and an Arabian ruler. It provided that 'the friendship of the two States may remain unshook to the end of time, and till the sun and moon have finished their revolving career' and, more practically, that an 'English gentleman of respectability' should reside in Muscat as British Agent. The first survived the climate for less than a year and it became regarded as certain death for Englishmen to attempt to pass the hot season there.

The history of the first half of the nineteenth century is dominated by the figure of Sayyid Said ibn Sultan who seized power in 1807, murdering a cousin in circumstances of exceptional treachery. His ambition was to dominate the East African coast and its trade and for this he needed British friendship. He made a point of receiving visiting Englishmen and usually contrived to charm them with his pleasant manners and by calling upon them in return. This could cause embarassment: in 1833 he announced his intention of inspecting HMS *Leven*, which carried several pigs as rations for the crew. It was felt necessary not to affront a Muslim ruler by their unclean presence so they had to be lowered into small boats: the unfortunate animals misunderstood the purpose of the proceedings and their protesting squeals, echoing back from the mountains, could be heard all over Muscat.

During the early years of his reign, Sayyid Said enjoyed the services as Commander in Chief and personal physician of a strange adventurer Vincenzo Maurizi, known locally as Shaikh Mansur. In the preface to his *History of Seyd Said*, Maurizi said that he had been born in Rome but had left Italy to avoid becoming involved in the civil strife which followed the French Revolution. In Constantinople he had doctored the Admiral of the Turkish fleet and fought at sea against the Russians. He then practiced in Cairo and Yemen before reaching Muscat. He paints an agreeable picture of the Omanis and in particular of Sayyid Said, one of whose banquets he attended. 'A long piece of calico was placed upon the ground, and upon this were laid a vast number of dishes of rich Chinese porcelain, containing fifty fowls roasted, many Dolma or messes of meat each wrapped in a leaf of the beet, which together with cabbage and spinage, is cultivated in almost every garden; plates full of ribs of mutton, etc. In the centre were two large wooden dishes, supporting lambs baked whole, and stuffed with rice; and to all these delicacies was added a great quantity of pillau.' After this one is surprised to read that 'excessive corpulence is unknown amongst the Arabs'. The evening concluded with fruit and party games.

Maurizi tells us that in Muscat there were sorcerers who could change a man into a goat and therefore in the *suq* it was necessary to look carefully for certain marks to avoid the possibility of buying someone who had fallen foul of a magician. Indeed, he says, his own servant once encountered a goat which had addressed him in Arabic. Maurizi may have been the first European to have penetrated far inland but unfortunately his projected second volume never appeared. He moved on to Baghdad where he again worked as a doctor, and then to Kurdistan where he commanded the artillery of a Persian prince. He was captured by the Russians in Azerbaijan but was soon released to resume his travels. He hints at secret missions in Teheran and subsequently worked in India and Brazil before returning destitute to Europe.

In 1835 Sayyid Said received the first American mission to visit Arabia. The warship bringing the envoy Edmund Roberts, ran aground off Masira and had to lighten itself by throwing overboard all its guns. The Sayyid won the Captain's gratitude by recovering them safely. The Americans were rather naive travellers: they apparently accepted without question Sayyid Said's yarn that Beduins fight by burying themselves up to their armpits and waving their swords above their heads. Like so many of their successors the Americans thought local methods of preparing food unhygienic: in particular they disliked the practice of stirring Halwa, the Arab sweet 'with the naked feet of sweating niggers' as they put it.

Sayyid Said was not alone in welcoming Europeans for on occasions his wife received visiting ladies. The first may well have been Mrs Mignan who, in 1825, passed the three padlocks, each a foot long, and the two handsome eunuchs who guarded the harem. She described the jewels worn by the Princess – an emerald the size of a pigeon's egg while pearls and diamonds covered her hands and feet. She was dressed in purple satin, richly embroidered, and wore 'a frightful thing, which re-

Pearling provided practically the only source of wealth for much of the southern Gulf before the discovery of oil. But even pearling failed with the invention of cultured pearls. The boatmen chanted as they rowed into port.

201

sembled a pair of broad-rimmed spectacles, but made of some kind of stiff cloth, richly worked and spangled with gold'. An Omani lady still assumes this mask at puberty and after this not even her own mother sees her without it.

So far Europeans had seen little beyond the town of Muscat but the first years of the nineteenth century brought them into close contact with the northern coast. The cause was piracy which had become acute since the conversion of the Qawasim tribe of Ras al-Khaimah to Wahhabism in the last decades of the eighteenth century: piracy had become invested with the aura of a Holy War and to attack Infidels became a positive duty. It was sinful, they were reputed to believe, to rob the living but there could be no objection to taking the property of the

Sail-making in Kuwait in earlier days.

dead: they therefore cut the throats of most of their captives. Their neighbours said 'their occupation is piracy and their delight is murder. They are monsters'.

Their attacks became more frequent and when there were Christian prisoners 'the Joasmi ladies were so minute in their enquiries that they were not satisfied without determining in what respect an uncircumcised infidel differed from a true believer'. Others were less fortunate: one British captain was chopped in pieces and thrown overboard while another had his arm severed but managed to staunch the bleeding by thrusting his stump into hot butter.

The first two expeditions against Ras al-Khaimah in 1809 and 1816 were ineffective and in the second practically the only casualty was a British sailor who 'was so much agitated by the sound of the discharge of the first gun, that he fell back and expired'. A third attack in 1819 finally broke the power of the pirates and for some months English soldiers were stationed at Ras al-Khaimah, using the mosque for church parades.

The General Treaty of Peace of 1820 started the process which changed the Pirate Coast into the Trucial Coast and visits by British officers became frequent. One of the earliest was Lieutenant Whitelock who described wrestling matches between the sailors and the Arabs. The latter, he said, 'wear their head-dresses hanging over in front very much, and it gives a scowl to their harsh rugged features which suits well with their characters'. However, 'quarrels are seldom heard of; old age is always respected; hospitality is proverbial; in manner they are stern, anything trivial or in the way of jokes or humour is either not understood or despised'. To one who has enjoyed the wit of the people of the Trucial States, this statement is strange: perhaps Whitelock's jokes were not very good.

This contact was still almost entirely confined to visits by sea: communication by land is difficult because of the *Sabkha* or salty marshes. Only one European seems to have gone inland before the end of the century and that was Captain Atkins Hamerton who went to Bureimi in 1840. He took four days to travel there from Sharjah and was impressed by the great fort which dominated the

Mrs Mignan's picture of the Sultana of Muscat, who received her in 1825.

left
This starched, beaky mask is still worn by ladies of the Arab Gulf states. It may occasionally, nowadays, even be seen in London.

oasis. It was equipped with guns whose origin nobody knew, but as there were no cannon balls their ammunition was stones and chunks of iron. He was astonished at the greenery – at the oranges, figs, pomegranates and olives as well as the magnificent palm trees and wheatfields. These were watered by *Qanats* – underground aqueducts with occasional shafts for ventilation and to permit the entry of repair workers. Some were of great length and one, he heard, extended fourteen hours from Bureimi. The local people, as so often in the Middle East, ascribed them to King Solomon: historians, however, are more inclined to think that Persians were responsible.

South of Muscat the British did penetrate, and with disastrous results. Captain Perronet Thompson, who had been left in charge of the force which had destroyed the pirates, was persuaded by Sayyid Said to use his troops to attack the tribe of Bani Bu Ali which had renounced its allegiance. In November 1820 over 500 men of whom nearly 30 were British, with a baggage train of 600 camels and 300 draft cattle started to march inland from Sur. Despite their superior armament and the help of the Sayyid's levies, they were utterly defeated by the savage *élan* of the tribal swordsmen. Seven English officers and 300 men were killed and a major punitive expedition was launched. In January 1821, 117 British officers, 1263 British Other Ranks and 1686 sepoys landed in Arabia. The Bani Bu Ali fought with desperate courage – one officer had his horse cut in half by a single sabre stroke – but the tribe was overwhelmed and its men taken into temporary exile. It was a lesson, however, that the British did not easily forget and an unwillingness to commit European troops in Arabia beyond the range of Naval guns was to dominate policy for another century and a half.

These brief adventures contributed little to knowledge of the interior of Oman but a great advance was made in 1835–6 through the exploration of James Raymond Wellsted. He was a naval officer and had taken part in the coastal surveys of Arabia, and was also probably the first to note down Himyaritic inscriptions which he had found at Husn Ghorab. Sayyid Said encouraged his wish to travel, presented him with a fine horse, a brace of greyhounds and a gold-mounted sword, and undertook to pay all his expenses. He was the first to discover the beauties of mountainous Oman, writing of the town of Minna, 'lofty almond, citron and orange-trees yielding a delicious fragrance on either hand, exclamations of astonishment and admiration broke from us. "Is this Arabia," we said "this country we have looked on heretofore as desert?" Verdant fields of grain and sugar-cane stretching along for miles are before us; streams of water flowing in all directions, intersect our path; and the happy and contented appearance of the peasants, agreeably helps us to fill up the smiling picture . . . I could almost fancy that we had at last reached that "Araby the blessed", which I had been accustomed to regard as existing only in the fictions of our poets.' It was not only the countryside that he admired for 'more frolicsome, laughter-loving dames I never beheld'.

He enjoyed the society of the local Arabs, happily ate

camel and roast sheep with them and taught his hosts how to play leapfrog. He was impressed by their hardihood and told of an ancient man, tormented with an internal complaint, who from time to time hurled himself from his camel and rolled on the ground in agony, never uttering a moan. He gave them pills of ambergris and opium which they hopefully regarded as aphrodisiac and in return sampled their wine, a mixture of grape and pomegranate juice which he does not recommend.

Starting in Bani Bu Ali, where he had a most friendly reception from tribesmen who had really quite enjoyed their exile, he travelled in a circle and regained the coast

A modern photograph of Muscat taken from the air, showing the spectacular setting. The Portuguese forts can be seen on the left.

at Sib, just north of Muscat. A few days later he set out again with four companions and five camels. His account of how these were hired show his gifts of observation and of narrative 'bargains usually commence in a low tone, by one party naming a price ten times greater than what he intends to take, or expects the other to give: a sneer, or stare of well-feigned astonishment, is the only answer: the debate gradually becomes warmer, and the parties shift their seat from one spot to the other. At one time old Ali's voice could be heard shouting high above that of his opponent; at another time, huddled together in some hollow, as if afraid the very winds might bear away some part of their counsels, I could just catch the sound of his voice, exerted in tones of pathos, reproach, expostulation or entreaty. At length he would start up and retire, breathing maledictions against their unheard-of rapacity, but followed by one or two bystanders who bring him back, when a repetition of the same scene occurs, until the affair is settled.'

Wellsted hoped to get through to Nejd but he failed to pass beyond Ibri. The people were hostile to a Christian and their objections to his presence were so strong that 'my interpreter, a Persian six feet high and stout in proportion, was so perfectly unmanned by his fears, that he went into fits'. Wellsted was pelted with stones and forced to retreat to the coast. It was a whole generation before another European got so far inland again.

He had the greatest of all gifts in an explorer – an intuitive understanding of the people that he met and a sympathy with them. Again and again his observations ring true. He saw the oasis dwellers as a 'proud, high-spirited race, less corrupted or degenerated than those who, in other parts of Arabia have passed from the pastoral to the agricultural state ... hospitable, brave, generous, but at the same time vindictive, irascible'. He admired the Beduin 'if we contrast [his] character in general with that of his neighbours, how immeasurably he stands before them! – his patriotism and natural independence render him as far superior to the Persian – a polished slave – whose best energies are chilled by despotism, – as his superior physical strength, hardihood, and courage, place him before the placid, mild, enervated Hindu . . . He believes himself to be the purest and best of mankind.'

Through the patronage of Sayyid Said, he travelled under the most favourable auspices and there is no doubt that he did almost as much for our knowledge of Oman as Niebuhr did for the Yemen. He admitted that he knew little Arabic and certainly he made mistakes in understanding what people said to him. His maps are not always accurate and he was not generous to his associates. Much of his second book, recounting a journey from Baghdad to Damascus, is told in the first person but is an account of a journey made by one of his friends. The tale of how he

Food on a desert journey. Nearly every Beduin can cut up and cook a carcass if he is lucky enough to obtain one. This photograph by Bertram Thomas shows a butchered goat being prepared for the pot.

was nearly killed by a fanatical mob in Damascus, of his unsuccessful loves for a Greek girl and for a Muslim widow may be pure fiction.

However his account of Socotra and of the Hejaz coast are of interest. Near Yanbu, he noted, 'the Arabs have a singular custom of making incisions almost to the quick in the soles of their feet, which they afterwards thrust close to the fire. This operation, aided by a few cups of coffee, mingled with spices and pepper, is pronounced to be an excellent preventative against the effects of the cold'. The end of Wellsted's life was tragic. He returned to Muscat in 1837, but, in a delirium of fever, fired two shots into his mouth. He lingered on for a few more years before dying at the age of thirty-seven.

Sayyid Said died in 1856 and after his death Muscat languished. Trade fell away as steamers replaced the Omani dhows and a visitor in the 1890s reported that much of the town was in ruins. There was civil strife, too, as the conservative Ibadhis of the interior opposed the changes that contact with the West was bringing to their cousins of the coastal area. In the general insecurity no one followed Wellsted into the interior and a scholar writing in 1870 complained that 'it is remarkable, and by no means creditable to the British Government in India that notwithstanding our intimate political and commercial relations with Oman for the last century, we know actually less of that country, beyond the coast, than we do of the Lake District of Central Africa'.

However between 1872 and 1886 the British Agent in Muscat was S. B. Miles whom we have already seen as the first explorer of the Aden hinterland. He was an excellent Arabic linguist and interested in everything. He noted, for example that a male palm tree may rise to 130 feet and that one is enough to fertilise some 700 females. Some trees acquire reputations as 'stallions' and their sprigs sell for several dollars. The females mature at eighteen years and then may produce up to 300 lbs of dates a year.

Miles followed in Wellsted's steps and more than once encountered old men who remembered the visit of the previous Christian forty years before. He was not stopped at Ibri, which he found 'dirty, malodorous, thronged with spare gaunt Beduins' all heavily armed; he became the second European to reach Bureimi and the first to approach it from the east. Like Hamerton, he was impressed by the greenery but, as his account was not official, felt able to record that the women wore high-heeled shoes and had black cloths over their heads instead of the masks of Muscat.

A quarter of a century elapsed before another westerner reached Bureimi and this time it was an American missionary, the Rev Samuel Zwemer who rode in from Abu Dhabi. He noted that his escorting Beduins refused to eat tinned food but preferred freshly-caught lizards with their rice. He praised the hospitality of the people and admired their tolerance for he was allowed to stay in the mosque and even to preach there. He reached the Batinah coast on the Gulf of Oman and calculated that the whole journey had cost him and his companions a total of $90.

Zwemer was quickly followed into Bureimi by Percy Cox, then British Agent in Muscat and later to win fame as High Commissioner in Iraq. He was escorted to the oasis by one of the sons of the Shaikh of Abu Dhabi – a bright lad with whom he discussed modern technology and the possibility of crossing Arabia by balloon. At this time the aeronaut, the Rev J. M. Bacon, had a plan to use the prevailing winds which blow from west to east to launch a balloon in the Sudan in the hope of reaching the Gulf. He had already crossed the Irish Sea in that way and on another occasion just missed a collision with St Paul's Cathedral.

Cox travelled on from Bureimi under Omani auspices. Occasionally he came under fire and discovered that etiquette demanded that if one was hostile, one returned the shots but otherwise ignored them. No one could remember having seen a Briton in Ibri before so the entire population insisted upon shaking hands with him. In Tanuf, however, he came upon a memory of Miles, who had been there twenty-five years before. The local shaikh claimed that there had been no rain since the Christian had taken photographs, and demanded compensation for his lost crops, a claim which Cox declined to honour. After two visitors in three years, Bureimi had to wait for

The Gulf is probably the oldest seaway in the world. Dhows like this Kuwaiti boom can still very occasionally be seen trading with India or East Africa.

another quarter of a century until an oil prospecting party went there in 1925. When Wilfred Thesiger arrived in 1948, it was still regarded as remote and inaccessible but in 1970 the present writer was taken there in an hour along a dual-carriageway from Abu Dhabi and shown the building which was to become the Hilton Hotel.

In 1894 the Bents, Mabel and Theodore, whom we met in the last chapter, visited Muscat and were received by the young Sultan. They noticed two cages in his palace: one contained a criminal and the other a lion. Some medical missionaries settled there in the same year, one of whom, the American Paul Harrison, gives an amusing picture of a doctor's life. A shaikh needing dental treatment brought along a slave on whom the doctor should show his skill before being permitted to operate on the great man's own mouth. A Beduin paid for some medicines by leaving his donkey which he subsequently stole back after the missionaries had fattened it. Harrison made several journeys inland along the precipitous tracks of Jabal Akhdar which Wellsted had previously

211

Bertram Thomas's photograph of himself—just about to start on the first crossing of the Empty Quarter.

left
Bertram Thomas and his companions.

described. He wondered at the sure-footedness of his donkey which climbed like a cat, often pausing to sniff out its path like a dog.

So far we have ignored the southern province of Oman, although in antiquity it was by far the most important: scholars indeed believe that Dhofar may well have been the Biblical Ophir. Early visitors, before the end of the seventeenth century, were British sailors who had been shipwrecked and they were treated with great hospitality. Later they learned that the event had been foretold by a religious leader, who had ordered the Beduins to protect them. They were taken overland to Muscat, fed on dates and camel milk: when they fell ill, the Arabs, anxious to do their best, cauterized them with hot irons.

Despite this, Ovington wrote some years later that the Dhofaris 'are very injurious in their Commerce and Villanous to strangers'. He went on to describe their religious activities: 'heated with extatick warmth, that they are not asham'd sometimes to pretend even to Inspiration, expecially when they are siez'd with a fit of

Dancing. For among them prevails a particular Custom of Dancing with so much pains and Zeal, so much fervency and Passion that their strength decays, and their Spirits fail them thro' these violent Motions, and being at length quite spent, they fall as it were quite dead upon the ground. All the while this merry Humour does possess them, they cry aloud "God is a great God".' We have seen, however, that unfortunately we cannot rely on the Rev Mr Ovington.

We hear little more about Dhofar until the 1830s, when the Indian Navy started to survey its coasts. One of the best accounts was that of Captain Haines who met among the tribesmen an American who had been captured by pirates thirty years before and who had settled as a Muslim with a local wife. He and the Arabs enjoyed watching the Britons playing cricket on the sands. Haines described the people of the region, the Qara, as a fine athletic race, most of whom were armed with a throwing stick which, rebounding along the ground, could kill at 100 feet. They were very hospitable and one of Haines' party who went a few miles inland was offered a wife and several sheep. His welcome was so great that he was never allowed to drink from the streams and whenever he attempted to do so, people rushed up with bowls of milk. Another officer described their pipes which were made of lime which gradually hardened, and their swords which, without scabbards, they always carried sloping over their right shoulders.

The first Europeans to go more than a few miles inland were the Bents in 1894. They stayed first with the tough Omani governor at Al Hafa where they found heavily fettered prisoners and others chained to blocks of wood who 'bewailed their misdeeds into the small hours of the night'. The governor provided them with an escort of seventeen shaikhs, whom they paid half a dollar a day but 'we never had to deal with wilder men in our lives than those who constituted our escort . . . Not a whit less wild than their masters are the camels of the Qara; they danced about like antelopes.' Mrs Bent recorded that Dhofari camels had a strong predilection for old bones and would dart from the track and start munching them whenever the opportunity offered. They were deeply impressed by the beauty of the country: 'that arid Arabia could produce so lovely a spot, was to us one of the greatest surprises of our lives'.

After this adventurous pair, there seems to have been no significant travel in Dhofar until the late 1920s. The Bents were very amateur: the next arrival was highly professional. Bertram Thomas had served as a Political Officer in Iraq before becoming in 1924 Wazir to the Sultan of Muscat, in whose company he made several journeys in the coastal areas of eastern Oman. He watched and recorded the customs of the people: he learned that illness can either be treated by swallowing the vomit of a cow obtained through ramming a stick down its throat, or by propitiating the *jinni* who lived in the spot where it was contracted by sending a virgin with the offer of an egg.

He recounted, too, the tale of a man who, despite his family's forgiveness, insisted upon expiating the murder of his uncle. Finally a shaikh decreed that he should walk backwards into a well which had been filled with sharp

A distant view of the Oman mountains, where Wellsted so enjoyed himself. Jabal Kaur, with Jabal Akhdar on the extreme right.

spikes. Unflinchingly he did so but at the last moment he was caught in the arms of his relatives.

Thomas's main objective was to cross the Empty Quarter, the Rub al Khali, and he was fortunate in having ample time to make his preparations. During the period 1927–8 he made a 600 mile camel ride in Dhofar and the following winter he rode northwards to the very edge of the great Sands. During these journeys he won the confidence of the tribesmen by behaving exactly as they did: he grew a beard, wore local dress, refrained from smoking and drinking and ate as they did. On occasions he came under fire with them. On his second expedition he arranged for tribesmen of the Al Rashid to meet him the following year to conduct him to a point where he could hope to meet Murra Beduins coming from the north.

At first it looked as if he would be disappointed for there were rumours of fighting and raiders: the Saar, wolves of the Empty Quarter, were believed to be on the warpath. However the party started off from Dhofar on 10 December 1930 and caught its first glimpse of the Gulf on 2 February. Thomas wrote of the Sands, 'very impressive is the great dune region at first sight – a vast ocean of billowing sands, here tilted into sudden frowning heights, and there falling into gentle valleys ... without a scrap of verdure in view. Dunes of all sizes, unsymmetrical in relation to one another, but with the exquisite roundness of a girl's breasts, rise tier upon tier like a mighty mountain system. No contrasting shades are afforded by the sun's almost vertical rays.' Again he wrote 'there were moments when we came suddenly upon a picture of sublime grandeur, an immense and noble plastic architecture, an exquisite purity of colour, old rose-red, under a cloudless sky and brilliant light. A winter's day in Switzerland affords a comparison – the feel of the yielding substance underfoot and a glorious exhilaration in the air.'

Subsequent travellers have shown that Thomas crossed the Empty Quarter by the easiest route – one which the Beduins use – but nothing can detract from his achievement. There had been moments of real danger with possible raiders but, as he said 'the sands are a public diary' and his escort could tell who was about from the tracks and even identify individual camels. Later Thesiger was to say that a Beduin could tell from the droppings exactly where a camel had last grazed and how long had elapsed since it had passed. Thomas heard, too, the roaring of the sands which he described as resembling a ship's foghorn and which lasted two minutes. The value of his work was enhanced by his excellent photography.

No one has contributed more to the knowledge of this part of Arabia than Thomas, for his range of interests was so wide. He collected folklore, telling us how the hyaena is a witch's camel, of how apes are descended from a man who stole the Prophet's sandals and how the black mark on the tail of a hare comes from Muhammad's hitting it with a charred stick because it delivered a message to the

The men of the Qara tribe still carry the throwing stick, with which Haines said they could kill at a hundred feet.

A Saar tribesman, one of 'the wolves of the Empty Quarter'.

wrong person. He was deeply interested in zoology and had alarming experiences as, for example, when a Beduin brought him in a five-foot cobra still very much alive. Even more interesting were his studies of the people who dwelled on the edges of the Sands and whom he regarded as survivors of the original pre-Semitic inhabitants of the Peninsula. He studied their strange languages, and this search took him also to Musendam – the peninsula of Oman pointing towards Persia – where he visited the Shihu troglodytes. He found them living in pits, twelve to fourteen feet deep; fifteen feet long and twelve feet wide. The side walls were of stone, and the roof of timber covered with sand so that their houses were barely visible. He also described their dancing: a dozen men stood in a circle, their leader howled while they answered him with doglike barks, before throwing their swords in the air and catching them with their bare hands. Thomas left Muscat in 1931 and later rendered valuable service as the first head of the School of Arabic Studies which is now at Shemlan in the Lebanon.

After the war Wilfred Thesiger started a series of crossings of the Empty Quarter, which took him to many places such as the Lewa where still no European had ever penetrated. He had started exploring while still an undergraduate, and as a District Officer in the Sudan, had made many long tours on camel back. After an adventurous war, he was employed by the Desert Locust Service – an organization which has done much for knowledge of Arabia.

His travels between October 1946 and May 1947 took him across the Empty Quarter from Salala to the Lewa and then in a semi-circle to Mukalla. He set off equipped with a camera, an aneroid, a press for plants, a small medicine chest, a volume of Gibbon and a copy of *War and Peace*. He took 2000 lbs of flour, 300 lbs of rice, some *samn* (clarified butter) and some coffee and tea. For meat the party depended on what it could shoot and vividly he describes their anguish when, after killing a hare, they encountered some passing Beduins with whom good manners demanded they should share it. Once a fox stole their gazelle meat during the night, but they found where

he had buried it, brushed off the sand and ate it with relish.

His team originally consisted of twenty-four men but most of these had to be dispensed with to save food and water, and the final group consisted of himself and four tribesmen, one of whom had previously crossed the Sands entirely alone. It was the comradeship of these men, and trying to understand them, that meant most to Thesiger. 'I felt affection for them personally, and sympathy for their way of life,' he wrote, and in another place he said, 'I craved for the past, resented the present and dreaded the future.' As 'hour after hour my camel shuffled forward, moving it seemed, always up a slight incline towards an indeterminable horizon', he obviously felt at peace. If anything troubled him it was the lack of privacy rather than the solitude.

Thesiger has brought back much Beduin lore and gives a picture of how men actually live in the desert. Some of his geographical descriptions are worthy of his predecessors: 'Ramlah al Ghafa was very beautiful. The great dune masses 400 to 500 feet in height were of a rich warm red, shot with silver and gold, and dotted with clumps of yellow flowering tribulus and the bright green of the abal bushes.' However, as he said 'to others my journey would have little importance. It would produce nothing except an inaccurate map which no one was ever likely to use . . . It was a personal experience, and the reward had been a drink of clean, nearly tasteless water. I was content with that.'

As we suggested in an earlier chapter, more people have gone to Arabia to discover themselves than have gone to explore the Peninsula. No man can pretend in the harsh sunlight or the brutal desert of Arabia; but in addition to learning about himself, a man may, as a bonus, encounter one of the most fascinating races that God has made. This will never be the same in the future for, as Thesiger says, many will come to Arabia to study 'but they will move about in cars and keep in touch with the outside world by wireless. They will bring back results far more interesting than mine, but they will never know the spirit of the land nor the greatness of the Arabs.'

Further reading

The main sources for this book are the narratives of the travellers involved. They can be found under the name of the author in the catalogue of any major library so it is not proposed to set them out here. The books mentioned below may be regarded as a guide to further reading.

Three books give a general picture of the developing exploration of Arabia:

D. G. Hogarth: *The Penetration of Arabia*. London, 1905
R. H. Kiernan: *The Unveiling of Arabia*. London, 1937
J. Pirenne: *A la découverte de l'Arabie*. Paris, 1958

The following chapters can be amplified by consulting these sources:
Niebuhr and his Companions.
Thorkild Hansen: *Arabia Felix*. London 1964.
Burckhardt.
Katharine Sim: *Desert Traveller*. London, 1969.
Burton. There are numerous books on Richard Burton.
Byron Farwell: *Burton*, London 1963 is as good as any.
Palgrave.
Mea Allen: *Palgrave of Arabia*. London, 1972.
Doughty.
D. G. Hogarth: *The life of Charles M. Doughty*. London, 1935.
Anne Treneer: *Charles M. Doughty*. London, 1935.
Philby.
Elizabeth Monroe: *Philby of Arabia*. London, 1973.
Travellers in the Hejaz.
Augustus Ralli: *Christians at Mecca*. London, 1909.
William Bankes: *Narrative of the Life and Adventures of Giovanni Finati*. London, 1830.
Travellers in Eastern and Northern Arabia.
Lord Lytton: *Wilfrid Scawen Blunt*. London, 1961.
N. N. E. Bray: *A Paladin of Arabia*. London, 1936.
Travellers in South-west Arabia.
De la Roque: *Voyage de l'Arabie Heureuse*. Amsterdam, 1716.
H. P. Palmer: *Joseph Wolff*. London, 1935.
Travellers in Oman.
C. D. Belgrave: *Pirate Coast*. London, 1966.

Acknowledgments

Photographs

M. L. Beazley, Barnet 38, 39 bottom, 103; Biblioteca
Ambrosiana, Milan 58; R. L. Bidwell, Cambridge 39 top,
42–43, 98–99, 106–107, 146, 154–155, 183; British Library,
London 17, 26, 128; British Museum (Natural History),
London 177; Courtauld Institute of Art, London 134,
196–197; John Dayton, London 91, 94; Lt.-Col. Gerald de
Gaury, Brighton 153 right, 157; Hamlyn Group Picture
Library 7, 15, 20, 22, 28, 32, 40, 45, 47, 48–49, 50, 54, 56–57,
62, 63, 66–67, 70, 77, 80, 86, 92, 124, 131, 132, 136, 148 left,
148 right, 149 top, 149 bottom, 152, 158, 162, 165, 168, 170,
173, 174, 181, 182, 186, 194–195, 204 right; Mansell
Collection, London 16, 18, 60, 180; Middle East Centre,
Cambridge 143, 184, 188–189, 202, 208, 212 left, 212 right;
John Murray, London 190 bottom; Government of Muscat
206–207; Musées Nationaux, Paris 153 left; National Portrait
Gallery, London 84, 135, 159; Paul Popper, London 11,
24–25, 30, 44, 65, 71, 81, 82, 100, 111, 115, 118, 121, 125, 127,
140, 145, 178, 198–199, 201, 204 left; Radio Times Hulton
Picture Library, London 14, 68, 74, 87, 101, 144, 188 top;
Saint Anthony's College, Oxford 96, 104–105, 108 top, 108
centre, 108 bottom, 112, 113, 160; Professor R. B. Serjeant,
Cambridge 34–35, 46, 102, 150–151; G. R. Smith, Cambridge
2–3; Tate Gallery, London 52; Alan Villiers, Oxford 55, 211;
H. Roger-Viollet, Paris 31, 137.

The illustration on page 76 is reproduced by permission of the
Director of the India Office Library and Records, London. The
photographs on pages 185, 190 top and 191 are reproduced
from Freya Stark, *Seen in the Hadhramaut*, John Murray,
London (1938), that on page 176 from Freya Stark, *Winter in
Arabia,* John Murray, London (1940) and those on pages 10,
214, 216, 217, and 218 from Wilfred Thesiger, *Arabian Sands,*
Longmans, London (1959).

Index